# Writing Clearly
## A Self-Teaching Guide

# Writing Clearly
## A Self-Teaching Guide

## Dawn Sova

**WILEY**

**John Wiley & Sons, Inc.**

For general information about our other products and services, please contact our Customer Care Department within the United States at (800) 762-2974, outside the United States at (317) 572-3993 or fax (317) 572-4002.

Wiley also publishes its books in a variety of electronic formats. Some content that appears in print may not be available in electronic books. For more information about Wiley products, visit our web site at www.wiley.com.

ISBN 0-471-17952-3

Printed in the United States of America

10  9  8  7  6  5  4  3  2  1

# Contents

# Introduction

Writing clearly takes more effort than speaking clearly, and it can be a more intimidating experience. Many eloquent and articulate speakers go to great lengths to avoid placing their thoughts in writing, because the written word is permanent and allows the reader time to analyze and assess. In contrast, spoken words, unless recorded, have short lives, and mistakes made when speaking are more readily overlooked and forgotten.

Many people wrongly believe that the nearly universal use of computers has decreased the need for polished writing skills. E-mail can be very casual among friends, but formal electronic correspondence requires the same rules of writing and need for clarity as the more traditional "snail mail." Because you can send messages instantaneously, corresponding via e-mail may even demand *more* skill. You are under greater pressure to express your thoughts clearly and correctly in the first version of an e-mail communication, since you may not have the opportunity to edit and polish the expression of your thoughts if your finger is too quick on the "Send" button. Not all e-mail providers offer the "Unsend" command, and those that do offer it only for communications between users of the same service.

Why teach yourself to write clearly? The reasons are many, both personal and professional. We all want to be understood by others, and developing writing skills aids in achieving that aim. Getting an idea across requires writing that is well organized, specific in expression, and appropriate for the recipient or audience. Making yourself understood also demands that you take the time to edit and revise, so that the intention of your writing is clear. Otherwise, misunderstandings can occur, some of which may be serious. Sweeping generalizations, unclear references, and garbled or incomplete details permit the reader to fill in the blanks—and distort your meaning. Sentence errors, incorrectly linked ideas, and careless punctuation serve to project an uncaring attitude and raise questions in the reader's mind regarding the credibility and capability of the writer. Academic and business writing that masquerades as friendly prose undermines both the ideas expressed and the writer's image of competence and capability, while the extensive use of jargon and overly technical language in writing not aimed at a specialized audience marks a writer as pompous and the writing as unapproachable.

None of these flaws alone will prevent your message from getting across, but each has the potential for confusing your reader and suggesting interpretations of the writing that you might never have intended. When several of these flaws appear in your writing, you run the risk of sending readers a skewed message.

Why take the time to write clearly? Your writing may be your first contact with others in many situations, and it may thus serve as the basis for their first impression of you. From the dreaded college application essay to job application letters and business communications, the words you place on paper inform others what and how you think. If you learn to write clearly, you will send the correct message to all of your readers.

# How to Use This Book

*Writing Clearly: A Self-Teaching Guide* is intended for anyone who wants to communicate effectively. The book takes a practical approach to writing: chapters focus on key steps in the writing process and offer opportunities for you to address specific writing functions. Exercises and self-tests are provided to assist you in assessing your strengths as a writer and identifying your weak areas. This allows you to focus your efforts on developing the skills that you lack or that need improvement.

The chapters are arranged to allow you maximum flexibility in following a writing self-teaching effort. Whether you are interested in beginning with the basic concepts of writing or are an experienced writer seeking to hone your skills in only one area, you will find clearly defined and supported examples to meet your needs. For writers who are interested in applying already well-honed skills, this book offers chapters that review various types of academic writing and writing for business and technology. These chapters identify the shared and differing skills demanded by each type of writing. They include examples and assistance in responding to the information (or test) essay question, writing the argumentative or persuasive essay, developing the research essay, reporting laboratory or scientific results, and writing business letters, memoranda, and technical reports and manuals. The examples are specific to each type of writing and contain an analysis of what makes one attempt better than another. The book also addresses virtual communication and contains a chapter segment to aid you in writing clearly in cyberspace.

The book is structured simply, to provide a step-by-step guide that is both helpful and interesting to writers of all abilities. Each chapter opens with an example containing the writing concepts reviewed within, followed by a list of objectives; the author's commentary appears within brackets in the example text. Subtopics are identified and clearly explained, and fill-in-the-blank examples with answers immediately follow to illustrate the specific concept of each subtopic. For exercises that require writing a paragraph or more, three horizontal lines are provided to trigger readers to use additional paper. Key points or memory devices appear as "Quick Tips" in individual boxes that make them easier to locate and help to focus the writer's attention. Each chapter ends with a self-test and answers to provide instant feedback. An appendix contains a detailed "Writing Checklist" to use in evaluating your writing. The items listed in the checklist are discussed throughout the book.

The goal of *Writing Clearly: A Self-Teaching Guide* is to make you comfortable with expressing yourself on paper—and to assist you in making the correct writing choices so that readers will understand what you seek to communicate.

# 1 Targeting Your Audience

*He [the writer] must teach himself that the basest of all things is to be afraid; and, teaching himself that, forget it forever, leaving no room in his workshop for anything but the old verities and truths of the heart, the old truths lacking which any story is ephemeral and doomed—love and honor and pity and pride and compassion and sacrifice.*
—William Faulkner, speech upon receiving the Nobel Prize (December 10, 1950)

*The writer's only responsibility is to his art. He will be completely ruthless if he is a good one. . . . If a writer has to rob his mother, he will not hesitate; the "Ode on a Grecian Urn" is worth any number of old ladies.*
—William Faulkner, *Writers at Work: The Paris Review Interviews* (1959)

## Objectives

In this chapter you will learn to:

- target the specific audience for your writing

- determine how much to tell your reader

- make your writing credible

The quotations that open this chapter express the role of the writer in society, each tailored to a specific audience with whom novelist William Faulkner sought to communicate. Faulkner was clearly aware of the differences between the two audiences. His Nobel acceptance speech was directed partly to nonwriters, and most who heard or read his speech were members of a distinguished group of scholars—scientists, economists, politicians, and authors of scholarly works. The tone of the quotation reflects this awareness, and Faulkner's sentiments and words are lofty and formal, as befit the occasion.

In contrast, his tone and word choice are colloquial when he describes the writer's role for the readers of the *Paris Review*—mostly fellow writers. He is free to refer to the "Ode on a Grecian Urn" and to expect that his audience will not only be familiar with the John Keats poem, but will know also its literary importance. The informal manner in which Faulkner makes his point exhibits his certainty that readers of the *Paris Review* are likely to be writers who share his point of view and understand his passion. Had Faulkner offered the Nobel committee the same observations, he might have been met with polite amusement and perceived as somewhat eccentric in his views. In a similar manner, readers of the *Paris Review* might have found his recommendation of "verities and truths of the heart," as well as his appeal to such finer emotions as "love and honor and pity and pride and compassion and sacrifice," maudlin and not worth listening to. Even the similarity of topic is not sufficient to make Faulkner's point clear to both groups without his modifying each message for the specific audience. Faulkner knew the effect that his words would have, and so he organized his ideas and expressed them in a manner to make each audience feel most comfortable. He could thus ensure that the members of each group would understand the meaning and intent behind his words.

The work of writing clearly is not always intended to appease audiences or to satisfy their needs. Rather, a writer's work is to make a point. Faulkner knew this as well, and in other instances he may have also known his audiences well and used that knowledge to manipulate them through his selection and handling of the subject matter. Thus he could choose to express perfectly his ideas to achieve whatever his desired end, whether to entertain, or to inform, or to incite so that communication with the reader might become so abrasive that all further attempts at interaction would be blocked. All writing has this potential.

Each time you write anything—whether it is one sentence or a tome—you must identify your readers and your relationship to them, determine how much they already know about what you are writing, and assess how to convince them that your writing is worth reading.

# Imagining Your Reading Audience

Good communication depends upon the interaction of what you write and your intended reader. Important ideas and the articulate expression of those ideas fail to come across if they are aimed at the wrong audience. Similarly, providing readers with more information than they want or need to know can be as detrimental to your goals as withholding necessary facts. The delivery of identical thoughts in different situations and to different readers requires that you individualize your delivery to take into account the many ways your ideas might be perceived and understood.

Of course, a writer is not required to know readers individually or at all, but most writers have at least a general audience in mind and a purpose when they put words on paper. The tone of the writing may be friendly and relaxed, provocative and accusatory, or informative and technical, and the details may be abundant or sparse, depending on the extent to which the writer perceives the reader to share similar beliefs, understanding, knowledge levels, and needs. Writers who misjudge their audiences may learn too late that their important messages have been ignored by readers who feel alienated by the form of delivery or who sense no rapport whatsoever with the writer. Audiences who require factual and technical information are unlikely to be satisfied by creative nonfiction writing, and readers who seek entertainment will avoid terse writing that instructs or informs. Read the following example and determine the audience for which it is written.

What has happened to the dress code that people in professions and business used to follow? We used to be able to tell a person's occupation by the way he or she dressed. Beauticians (now "hairstylists") wore clean white uniforms and polished white shoes. Every hair on their head was in place. They were not permitted to chew gum while working on their clients' hair. Doctors would wear white coats or jackets while taking care of patients in their offices or making rounds at the hospital. Priests were never seen in public unless they were wearing their white clerical collars and black shirt and pants. Secretaries wore suits or blouses and skirts to the office and their clothing reflected their pride. Clothing salesclerks served as good advertisements in clothing stores for which they worked, for they often dressed to the level of their surroundings. Even housepainters proudly wore their uniforms of white coveralls and caps, which would remain largely free of spatters if the painter were experienced in his work. Times have really changed, and I do not think the change is for the better. People in all occupations should take more pride in their positions, and companies should demand this pride. Maybe a recession is not such a bad idea, because it may make people more attentive to looking and being their best.

This paragraph can serve any number of purposes, from providing a historical examination of the world of work to serving as an editorial commentary on the lack of pride among workers today and the role played by the economy. The writer must keep in mind that the issue of dress codes in schools remains a hotly debated topic, but general society has largely come to accept jeans and other casual clothes as a uniform for hairstylists, doctors, and housepainters, as well as less polished images for secretaries and salesclerks. The opinions expressed by the writer also suppose a certain rapport with the reader, who is expected to share the writer's approval of the dress codes of old.

What reading audience would be most likely to understand the writer's point and relate to the position taken in the final two sentences? Clearly, this writing is directed at older readers who have lived through the period in which dress codes for these occupations were commonplace and who share the same sense of social norms that the writer implies.

This does not mean that only an individual reader known to the writer or readers who are the same age as the writer will sympathize with the additional ideas that follow this paragraph. A wider audience made up of readers interested in the past would also appreciate the writer's reminiscences. This paragraph might also be part of an editorial writing that would draw readers who are not bound by age or experience but by a common goal related to the issue of dress codes. Before we can identify with certainty the audience for this writing, further

---

┌─────────────────────────────────────────────────────────────┐
│ ▭══ **QUICK TIP** ■═══▷

# Become Your Reader

Role-play and pretend to be your reader when placing words on paper.
If you find your explanation unclear, so will your reader.
└─────────────────────────────────────────────────────────────┘

details must be provided and the ideas must be more fully developed to appeal more completely to a specific audience.

**SELF-TEST**

Consider the sentences below and determine the audience for each. Does one sentence make its point more clearly than the others? As a critical reader, do you find that one sentence works better than another? Do you identify more closely with one sentence than with the others?

Before you can answer these questions, as the potential writer of such sentences, you have to become the reader and decide what the writer of each sentence seeks to communicate. All of the sentences share a common topic—the building in the center of town—but the presence or absence of certain details, the writer's choice of vocabulary, and the tone of each suggest that different readers are targeted by each sentence.

Match each sentence below with one of the following possible readers, and explain your choice:

1.  A centrally located structure of considerable height serves as the source of a satisfying representation of the character of this select corner of the region.

2.  A picture of the tower in the middle of town would be a good memento of your trip to this city.

3.  Power and dominance are expressed symbolically in the forty-story concrete and steel office building that stands far above its wood and brick neighbors, none of which extends farther than four stories toward the sky.

4.   The tower building is located at 435 Main Street in the center of the business district.

5.   Situated on two city lots measuring 60 feet by 125 feet, the tower building is set 12 feet from each side boundary, 18 feet from the public curb, and 30 feet from the rear boundary line.

a.   individual reading a survey of the property

b.   person reading directions

c.   tourist or casual visitor

d.   political or social observer

e.   professional painter or photographer

## ANSWERS

1—e.   The reader is a professional painter or photographer whose interest lies in viewing objects as representing more than their simple physical presence. The writer's language suggests that the tower will offer the reader an artistic perspective, which is "satisfying," in an area that is "select."

2—c.   The reader is a tourist or visitor to the specific area. The writer's language is casual and informal yet informative, and it suggests that only the existence of the tower is important to the reader, not the physical details or the symbolic value.

3—d.   The reader is a political or social observer who may also be an academic scholar, written to by the same. The writer's language is informative, yet it is also infused with opinion that may be interpreted as political or social commentary, as the tower is associated with "power" and "dominance" and contrasted with its less sturdily built and shorter neighbors.

4—b.   The reader is someone needing directions. The specific and brief statement that includes a street address and site locator—"in the center of the business district"—suggests a reader who is not taking the time to locate tourist sites. Instead, the reader of this example seeks specific information.

5—a.    The reader of this example is interested in the type of information usually found in a land survey or deed and may be a surveyor, a buyer, or a seller of a piece of property. The specific dimensions of the land and the exact measurements of the placement of the tower create a businesslike tone and suggest a professional reader.

# Deciding What Your Audience Needs and Wants to Know

Information overkill is as much a roadblock to writing clearly as is vague generalization. Writing that tells specific readers more than they need to know about a topic obscures the writer's message and may even result in confusion. Readers overwhelmed by information are forced to determine what may or may not be important to them and to block out what appear to be unnecessary details and extraneous information. A danger lies in providing more information than an audience requires, because an audience reading to learn more about a topic is seeking information from the writer and does not have the knowledge to separate necessary facts from uncalled-for details. Nor should they. In short, a writer who overwrites is inconsiderate of the reading audience and risks boring or confusing—not informing—them.

Consider the excerpt below, an answer to the following essay test question asked of students in a college history course: "What antiwar actions were taken in the United States by protestors against the Vietnam War?"

Those who protested against American military action in Vietnam in the 1960s and 1970s had many ways to show just how dissatisfied they were with their country. Television news showed numerous acts of draft card burning and even burning of the United States flag in protest. Many people joined what was called the "Peace Movement," which organized marches, passed out antiwar flyers, and spoke out loudly wherever it found listeners. Radical groups within the antiwar effort chose to punish the United States by creating destruction at home. In addition to funding mass demonstrations, these organizations also spawned groups within that attacked government buildings, bombed symbols of American capitalism, and robbed banks. They claimed to be performing such illegal and dangerous acts as a protest against the American "military-industrial complex" that they said was really the aggressor in Southeast Asia. *Many Southeast Asians and people of Southeast Asian descent in the United States did not appreciate the efforts that the United States government made in Vietnam. They saw the destruction of their homeland or ancestral land as wasteful and doing more to harm than to help those in the country. Other nations, as well, disapproved of what our country was doing, but not all spoke up at the time. It is only in recent years that the extent of disapproval regarding the efforts of the United States in Vietnam has been revealed.*

The writer of the this paragraph provides a focused answer to the question until halfway through the response. The section in italics takes the response into a completely new direction, although the writer seems unaware of the change in focus. In the first six sentences, the reader learns of specific actions taken by individuals and organizations in the United States who protested the Vietnam War, information required by the question. The seventh sentence and those following it identify and discuss the way in which people other than the antiwar protestors viewed the actions of the United States. Although the issue of dissent is generally the topic of both sections of this response, the original question clearly requires the identification of actions occurring in the United States only. The observation that other nations disapproved of United States military action may be accurate and interesting, but it is unnecessary and detracts from the precise information required by the question. The writer would have performed a greater service for readers by providing further relevant examples or by adding details to the examples given.

Vague generalizations also detract from clear writing, because readers who are given too little information are forced to fill the void with their own suppositions, which may not agree with the writer's intentions. At best, writing that is too general will simply waste the time of readers. At

---

**◁▭▭ QUICK TIP ▬▬▷**

## Be Considerate of Readers

Give readers the information that they need and present it in a form that they can understand. Too much information is as useless as too little.

worst, a writer's specific message will become distorted, and the resulting damage will mean both lost or inaccurate information for the reader and distrust of the writer, who will appear to have misled readers.

Consider the following paragraph, which appeared as an activities announcement in a college newspaper:

> Everyone on campus should support National Coming Out day, because we could all enjoy a little more tolerance in our lives. People are people and no one should think otherwise, no matter how others spend their personal time. This campus celebration will bring a new awareness to students and faculty, who will see that we are just like anyone else. Activities have been designed to fully involve all facets of the campus and to bring us all together, no matter how we think. Opening ceremonies will begin at 9 A.M. in front of the student center with the raising of the LGB flag and speeches, then continue throughout the day at various points around campus.

Does the writer fulfill the requirements of a writing that is intended as an "activities announcement"? What information does the announcement provide? What vital information does it omit? Who is the audience?

The writer deprives readers of most of the necessary information that should appear in an activities announcement. Even though "everyone" seems to be the audience, the real audience might be anyone who is interested in either taking part in activities for National Coming Out Day or who supports the day of acknowledgment. The specific activities should be identified, with their appropriate locations and times. The writer should not use the announcement space to editorialize about lifestyle issues. Expressing an opinion such as "we could all enjoy a little more tolerance in our lives" is inappropriate in an announcement of this type—as is expressing any opinion. The writer of an announcement is providing information, and the expected audience is seeking information and fact, not opinion.

**SELF-TEST**

The paragraph below is taken from instructions for assignments that a teacher of high school Advanced Placement English left for a substitute teacher.

### Assignment Due at the End of Class

Students are to select one of the following writing topics and to produce a written response that comprehensively exhausts all possible avenues of discourse. Students may draw upon their readings in this class, as well as their readings outside of this class and their experiences in life. You might be interested in knowing that, to this point in the year, students have been required to read *Demian* by Hermann Hesse, *Crime and Punishment* by Fyodor Dostoyevsky (alternate spellings exist), *Hamlet* by William Shakespeare, *The Importance of Being Earnest* by Oscar Wilde, and *The Fountainhead* by Ayn Rand, as well as a range of poets, both ancient and modern. They have also been instructed to read the *New York Times* each Sunday, and to pay particular attention to the book review section. Several of the students are avid readers and may surprise you with the extent of their knowledge, but do not feel intimidated by them. They are really nice students, and, because they do not expect much of substitute teachers, you can simply read my instructions to them and let them work on their own. I have left similar instructions and had excellent results in the past. As a further reminder, please tell students that this is the usual 1,000-word, coherent, well-organized, and grammatically perfect essay. Do not bother to read through the essays or to offer any comments on them, as I am particular about the types of responses given to my students' work. You may leave the completed work in my mailbox.

Is the writing level appropriate? Is the subject accurately addressed? Are sufficient details provided? Are too many details provided? Is the writer considerate of the audience?

_____

_____

_____

### ANSWER

The writing sample above contains a large number of obstructions to good communication and requires drastic editing and revision if the writer is to be successful. In this situation, the reader is a captive audience who must fulfill the obligations of a substitute teacher in a school district in which the usual classroom procedures must be followed when the full-time teacher is absent. Therefore, a substitute teacher who wants to be called back to work in the district will follow these instructions, despite the derogatory tone and the excess of needless details.

The writing is faulty in two areas: (1) the choice of language is insulting to the reader, and (2) a lack of details to support the reason for the writing weakens its purpose. The overall tone of the instructions is unnecessarily pompous and condescending. The full-time classroom teacher speaks down to the substitute at the outset by using overly formal language in the phrase "comprehensively exhausts all possible avenues of discourse," rather than stating simply that the responses should be complete. The writer also appears to suggest, in such phrases as "You might be interested in knowing" and "may surprise you with the extent of their knowledge," that the substitute teacher will be impressed with the student reading list. The most blatant indications that the full-time teacher has little respect for the reader appear in her parenthetical comment that Dostoyevsky's name is spelled in various ways and in her recommendation that the substitute not feel intimidated by the students, as well as her seemingly insincere assurance that "they do not expect much of substitute teachers." She also insults the abilities and the intelligence of the reader by writing, "Do not bother to read through the essays or to offer any comments on them, as I am particular about the types of comments given to my students' work." Most of the statements fail to provide clear directions, instead serving only to obscure the important information that should be furnished.

All of the phrases identified above are irrelevant to the purpose of the writing, which should be to clearly and methodically provide directions for a student writing assignment. The writer's comments regarding the abilities of the students might simply have been intended to express her pride in their skills and knowledge, but her manner of expression does more to insult the substitute than to indicate her pride in her students.

In addition to its string of irrelevant details, this writing fails to focus adequately on the task for which it was composed—to provide assignment directions. To fulfill that obligation, the instructions should provide the substitute teacher with details regarding the nature of the assignment, requirements of format and word count, and the location of writing paper or reference books. They should also specify any limitations to be imposed on the students and indicate what to do with the papers when they are completed. Rather than tell the reader that she is "particular about the types of responses given to my students' work," the writer should request directly and without explanation that the substitute place no marks on the paper, since that is reasonable and implies nothing derogatory about the reader's abilities. In contrast, the wording of the instructions suggests that the substitute teacher is not capable of providing responses that would meet the presumed high standards of the full-time teacher.

A more reader-friendly version of the assignment instructions appears below, in an edited version that provides the substitute with necessary details while including only a minimum of editorializing.

### Assignment Due at the End of Class

Students will complete in class a writing based on one of the following topics, which you will place on the board. Remind students that their responses should follow the usual standards in regard to the thorough development of ideas, coherence, strong organization, and correct grammar. Support for their ideas should be drawn from their readings both in and out of class and from their life experiences. The responses should be approximately 1,000 words long. These students are self-starters and do not need much monitoring, so simply give them my instructions and the topic and let them work on their own.

Please collect the writings at the end of class but do not grade them. You may leave them in my mailbox at the end of the school day.

Review the changes in language between the two versions, and observe that the second communicates with, rather than condescends to, the reader. The second set of instructions has a businesslike tone and the directions are to the point, yet the reader expects the professional efficiency that it conveys and does not have to contend with disparaging comments.

# Gaining Credibility with Your Audience

Writers are often told to write about what they know, but many of us realize that such advice is not as straightforward—nor as restrictive—as those who advise would have us think. Every experience, interaction, and encounter we have and everything we hear, see, and read adds to what we "know." Writing well about a vast number of topics may be easy. The challenge lies in making others believe that what we write is valid and that we are fully qualified to express our thoughts and to provide accurate information. If you do not make yourself credible, readers will not place any value on your writing and they will tune out any message that you seek to communicate.

Gaining credibility with an audience does not require that a writer become a renowned authority on a topic, but it does require proof that the writer knows and understands a topic and has the qualifications needed to convey information about it to readers. Examples of credible writing range from a student's response to an essay examination question, to a book that examines a medical issue, to numerous types of magazine and newspaper articles in between. What must a student writer do in order to be viewed as credible? At the bare minimum, the student must have fulfilled course requirements; a professor will tend to view with skepticism a lengthy, detailed response from a student who was not enrolled in the course, or who failed either to attend or to complete the course readings. In such a case, the student's credibility will be in question, no matter how accurate the essay examination response might be. In short, the student writer must exhibit some means of preparation and some actual knowledge.

In the professional arena, appropriate preparation, training, and experience are the key criteria for assessing the credibility of a writer. Before accepting and applying the views and advice contained in any writing, you should first determine the writer's qualifications. Writing that presents medical advice provided by someone who is not a physician or other medical professional should be viewed with skepticism and as less credible than information on medical topics written by an educated professional with experience in such matters. Credibility remains an issue unless the writer levels with readers and presents significant evidence that the material in the book is based on interviews with medical specialists and comprehensive research, and that the

> ◢▬▬▯ QUICK TIP ▬▬▶
>
> ## Be a Credible Writer
>
> Write about topics with which you are either thoroughly familiar or can research by conducting interviews or visiting databases. Do not misrepresent yourself to readers.

writer's qualifications lie in the ability to sift and sort through the information to provide a coherent account.

The issue of strained credibility also extends to personal writing that seeks to share feelings or impressions but not necessarily to impart vital information. Consider the example of a writer who chooses to convey the agony of losing a child without having had children and without having suffered the loss of a child. The writer will not be viewed as credible by readers because the necessary experience is lacking. The most sensitive of portrayals in this case will be perceived as fiction. However, a writer in this situation can gain credibility by interviewing those who have suffered the experience and obtaining opinions and impressions with quotations from such individuals, as well as from those who counsel families who have suffered such a loss.

To gain credibility with readers, you must have the qualifications that make you an authority on a given topic, or establish for readers that you have become an authority on the topic through research and interviews with experts.

Establishing credibility is less difficult than it appears, as long as you are reasonable regarding what you claim to know and what you seek to have readers believe.

**SELF-TEST**

Read the following excerpt and determine what qualifications the writer must have to make the writing appear credible to you. Try to separate your own experiences or memories of other accounts from those stated in the work to provide as objective an analysis as possible.

Consider what you feel the writer should possess in the way of personal experiences, education, and state of life to make the information in the writing valid.

### Life in an Early-Twentieth-Century Immigrant Family

My, how the times have changed since the 1920s and 1930s in the United States. Years ago, a person paid 30 cents per pound for the best cut of steak, 9 cents for a quart of milk, one penny per hard roll, 20 cents for a pound of butter, 18 cents for a pound of hot dogs, and a penny each for doughnuts. Families could rent an apartment containing four rooms for $20 per month. These were "cold-water flats," where residents had to supply their own heat and hot water. Landlords made certain that a family moved into a clean, well-maintained, and freshly painted apartment, but they also had specific demands. The rules were very strict. No noise, not too much company, and rent was paid once a month and on time. Landlords kept duplicate keys and also reserved the right to check the rooms whenever they chose, to make certain that tenants were keeping the premises clean. The rights that tenants demand today were not dreamed of. Before landlords agreed to rent an apartment, they would ask how many people were in the family and demand to know where the person paying the rent was employed. Potential tenants were told whether they would be allowed to have others stay with them and for how long, if at all. No leases were signed, and instead arrangements were on a month-to-month basis, with rent paid by cash only. Tenants agreed to meet these requirements because apartments were scarce. They knew that tenants who crossed the landlord would find their furniture out in the street before they had the chance to pay the next month's rent.

**ANSWER**

What qualifications must the writer of the this account have to be credible? The obvious answer is that the writer should be an immigrant or a child born to immigrants and should have lived in the United States during the period identified and experienced the events described. The casual tone and the attention to specific details in the account suggest that the writer is very comfortable with the topic, but such comfort might be the result of hearing stories told repeatedly by elders or the product of extensive reading and research about life among immigrant populations in large cities.

To establish credibility, the writer should identify the source of the account in the early sentences. Did the writer live through the experiences? If so, then adding the following sentence, for example, would reassure readers of the writer's credibility: "Life has changed considerably since the 1920s, when I was a child, living in Passaic, New Jersey, with my parents, who were immigrants from Poland." What follows is now accepted as being a firsthand account and a collection of reminiscences, rather than a fictional version of life in "the good old days."

A writer who has not lived through the experience also has means of establishing credibility, and should take pains to do so at a similarly early point in the writing. How was the information gathered? Were interviews the source of the information, in the form of reminiscences by someone who had the experience? Did the writer conduct archival research? Or is the account a product of childhood memories and of listening to adults discuss their experiences as immigrants living in the United States in the 1920s and 1930s?

Whatever the source, the writer should inform readers at the outset. One sentence preceding the account will be sufficient. Following are examples with comments and suggestions placed in brackets, that writers can use to provide readers with information about their sources:

1.  "The experiences of the children of immigrants remain fresh in their minds more than seven decades later."

2.  "The archives at Ellis Island [*or any other data bank or research source*] abound with sharply etched memories preserved on tape and in writing for generations to come."

3.  "The yearning today for 'the good old days' seems a little misplaced, if the experiences of my parents are any indication. Times and prices have changed, but, in many ways, the past is no better than the present—only different." [*The writer, in this situation, would then edit the first line of the current account to reflect*

*the source: "Times have changed significantly in the United States since the 1920s and 1930s, when my parents were children, and I often think of the stories that I grew up hearing when adults gathered and reminisced about their early days as children of Polish immigrants living in the big city of their new land."]*

---

## To Communicate Successfully

1. Take your reader's perspective to judge your writing and the information you provide.
2. Treat your readers with consideration by giving them only the information that they need and phrasing it in language they can understand.
3. Be honest with your readers to establish your credibility.

---

**CHAPTER SELF-TEST**

Below is the body of a letter sent to a customer relations office of a large electronics firm by a disgruntled consumer whose CD player failed to perform to expectations. As you read the passage, assess how effectively the writer has communicated the problems with the product, whether the writer has dealt fairly with the reader in presenting the details of the problem, and how successful the writer is likely to be in achieving a resolution of the situation.

I recently bought a piece of junk CD player made by your company that worked only a week before it began to give me problems. Your company really took me for a ride and wasted my money, which I can hardly afford. The player doesn't play, and I can't figure out why, although I have tried hard to make it work.

I'm really sick of this happening over and over again. How often will I have to spend good money for a product that fails to work for more than a few days? If you don't do something about this problem immediately, I intend to consult my attorney to sue the XYZ Corporation. Please provide your response in writing, because I do not want to waste my time on telephone calls.

What changes should the writer make in the letter to more successfully communicate with the customer relations office? What information must the writer provide to achieve a satisfactory resolution of the problem? How can the writer project a more credible image as a wronged consumer?

_____

_____

_____

## ANSWER

This letter is typical of many consumer complaint letters received by companies in the United States and around the world. Rather than communicating the specific problems with the CD player and offering solutions, the writer only expresses feelings of anger and frustration. Instead of calmly providing the reader with facts, the writer rants, raves, and threatens, and greatly reduces the possibility of obtaining any immediate action. The most a customer service department can do when it receives a letter of this sort is to follow up with another letter, because the consumer has demanded that all communication occur by mail.

The answer lies in acknowledging that the reader is not responsible for the writer's difficulties and in providing complete and specific information, such as the model number of the CD player, the place of purchase, the specific manner in which the unit is malfunctioning, what efforts have been taken by the writer to make the CD player work, and suggestions for satisfactory solutions to the problem. Attacking the image of the company, expressing disgust for the consumer products industries, and threatening to sue are not productive. The writer's credibility, already weakened by the indication that many other products have similarly failed once the writer has purchased and tried to use them, is further impaired through the use of unsupported threats. In short, the letter provides the reader with no information regarding how the company may assist the writer, the original intent of the attempt at communication.

In chapter 2 we move from targeting an audience to developing the most effective techniques for deciding on a topic, selecting a focus, and determining how best to organize material in order to clearly communicate your thoughts.

# 2 Finding and Writing the Topic

## Objectives

In this chapter you will learn to:

- ask questions that aid in formulating your topic

- cluster ideas effectively

- create a strong thesis statement

- organize information for most effective expression

The introduction and specific ideas that will be discussed in any type of writing are hardest to determine at the outset, whether the writer has been assigned a specific topic or given free rein. Even when we know what we must write, selecting an approach, deciding how much and what type of information to include, and determining how to organize the material can pose serious obstacles to beginning the writing process. Some writers use the "blank slate" approach and simply sit in front of a blank piece of paper (or blank computer screen) and wait for the words to appear magically. Others practice freewriting, in which they allow their minds to roam and then write down everything that comes into their minds about a topic in a given time, usually ten to fifteen minutes.

Still others swear by the methodical creation of an outline and the stockpiling of ideas that relate to each entry in it.

Professional writers and others who write frequently use all three methods, because they know that no single method is effective for all writers and, just as important, that the same method may not be effective for one writer in all writing situations. Knowing when to use one method or another is an important ability in learning to write clearly.

# Asking Questions

To generate a specific topic—or to develop a pool of ideas that you will expand, or from which you will choose to support your generalizations—write a series of questions related to the task. You can use the "blank slate" approach, freewriting, or a methodical outline to determine the questions.

Whichever approach you choose, you must ask yourself a few questions first. What does a reader *need* to know about your topic? What information *must* you provide in order to communicate your thoughts clearly? What information do you *want* to provide to your readers?

Place yourself in the reader's role to create questions that, when answered, will result in fully developed, well-organized writing on your subject. Some of the questions may be very general, while others may be specific, but do not distinguish among them at this point. Just list all that come to mind.

You will later answer your questions by listing as many phrases, words, or complete thoughts as you can next to or beneath each of the questions. At this point, you should not strive to establish a coherent pattern of questions nor to provide a sophisticated collection of responses. Your goal is simply to create a list of questions that connect loosely to one topic and that will allow you a sufficient range of possibilities from which to develop your writing. Later you will identify how to cluster your topics to create relationships among them. This technique will aid you in writing a more coherent, better-supported response.

Some of the questions will have only one answer because they are so specific. Others may pose problems because they offer so many possibilities, and you will have to set boundaries regarding how extensive your brainstorming should be.

Consider the following example and decide which questions you must ask and answer to provide the most clear and credible explanation for your reader. A friend has asked that you write and explain why you have chosen to purchase one computer system rather than another. Listed below are questions that the reader must have answered and questions that the writer considers important to providing an accurate response. Several of the questions can answered in different ways, depending upon the technical knowledge of the reader.

Before you create a response, ideally you should know exactly how well the reader understands the technical requirements of computer systems, so that you can decide if your explanation should include a detailed identification of the hardware features, or if the reader will only be interested in such issues as price, availability, reliability, and personal preference. This is not always possible, so the questions that you ask must also include questions related to the reader's knowledge. As the writer, you must also anticipate the reader's questions in formulating a reply that is thorough and helpful.

1. What was the price of the system?

2. How much computer literacy do I need to fully use the system?

3. How long can I expect to keep the system?

4. What are the features of the system?

5. How long is the warranty?

6. Why did you select the specific computer system?

7. Where did you buy the computer system?

8. What type of technical support accompanies the system?

9. How much memory does the system have?

10. To what extent can upgrades be made to the system?

11. What limitations, if any, exist in regard to adding peripherals?

12. Does the system have networking capabilities?

13. Does the company offer a trade-in plan?

14. What are the Web capabilities of the system?

---

┌─────────────────────────────────────────────────────────────┐
│ ▭▭▭▭◲ **QUICK TIP** ▬▬▬▬◲
│
│ # Ask Questions to Find Your Topic
│
│ Decide what you would want to know if you were the reader, and
│ what you want the reader to know. Create questions that you will
│ answer in your writing.
└─────────────────────────────────────────────────────────────┘

Which questions would you want to have answered if you were the reader?

_____

What questions do you as the writer believe are important to answer in your response?

_____

Which questions have several possible answers?

_____

The reader would probably want answers to questions 1–8, and the writer would find answers to questions 9–14 of additional importance in providing a thorough response. Questions 2, 3, 6, 10, 11, and 14 have several possible answers, depending on the technical knowledge of the reader and the writer.

**SELF-TEST**

Read the following essay assignment and decide which questions your writing must address in order to communicate your thoughts effectively. List the questions that you would wish to have a writer answer if you were a member of a college admissions committee reading and reviewing the application. Also list the questions that you believe are critical for you to answer in order to display your best effort and to make the necessary good impression on the admissions committee.

Identify the person or event that has been the most important influence on your life. Explain what makes that person or event unique in your life.

**ANSWER**

The list below contains questions that are very general in nature, as well as questions that are very specific. Some have several possible answers, while others can only be answered in one way. All, however, must be considered when writing an essay on this topic for a college admissions application. Most of the questions relate directly to the content of the later essay, and listing plausible answers and thinking them out thoroughly will provide you with a strong foundation for a very well written essay.

1.  What are the events that have most changed your life?

2.  Who are the people that have had the most influence on your life?

3.  What represents a change or influence on your life?

4.  How much of a role have you played in effecting these changes?

5.  What are considered admirable or worthy life-changing events?

6.  What influences are most admirable or worthy?

7.  When did the events that influenced you occur?

8.  When did you meet or how long have you known the person who influenced you most?

9.  Why was the event or the person an important influence?

10.  How honest should you be in responding to the essay?

11.  How honest does the admissions committee expect you to be?

12.  Why would the question appear on a college admissions application?

Questions 5, 6, 10, 11, and 12 will not be addressed directly in the essay, but they are very important and should be given as careful attention as the remaining questions, 1, 2, 3, 4, 7, 8, and 9. You owe yourself the right to determine what would be the best information to provide and how you can best present it.

Why does this sort of question appear on a college application form? If you feel that the purpose is to trick you or to surreptitiously probe your subconscious, you will write in a different manner than if you view the question as just one of many challenges to face in the college application process. Deciding what and how much to reveal is also wise, and questions such as 10 and 11 permit you room for speculation and the means to evaluate your information. Although questions 5 and 6 might be considered dishonest and suggest that a student would write to impress the admissions committee rather than tell the truth, considering and trying to answer them are important because they are questions that many students who apply to colleges ask. The point is to avoid becoming obsessed with such questions, yet to use them in some manner in the writing.

# Clustering and Branching Ideas

The method outlined above, asking questions to create a list of details to organize into subtopics in your writing, may not work with all topics. Even those topics that seem to develop well from the listing method might produce further details or strong relationships among ideas when a process we'll call clustering or branching is used. In addition to eliciting new ideas and new combinations of ideas, clustering and branching provide ways of connecting related ideas. The writer is also able to decide in the planning stages whether or not one or more subtopics are worth pursuing and whether enough of a relationship exists among ideas to include them in the writing.

To use the *clustering method,* you must first decide on a topic, which you will write in the center of a circle on a sheet of paper. From that circle, draw lines that link to other circles, some smaller and some the same size, into which you will write ideas that are of the same importance as the topic, as well as ideas that are more specific. If an idea is more general than the topic about which you are writing, reject it, because your goal is to explore ideas to explain the topic further, not to use the writing to explore an issue that is larger and more comprehensive than the topic. Consider the smaller ideas to be satellites of the larger topic and place them surrounding the topic with that in mind. If one or more of the satellite topics can be divided into additional specific subtopics, create another level of the diagram with smaller satellites connecting to a subtopic to form additional clusters.

Review the sample writing in chapter 1 on the need for a dress code in various occupations (pp. 7–8). How can you use clustering to develop the topic into a longer writing? What relationships can you develop among the existing ideas? Which ideas are major ideas that will develop into satellites of their own, and which are minor ideas that will remain undeveloped and perhaps might be discarded?

The corresponding diagram should look something like this:

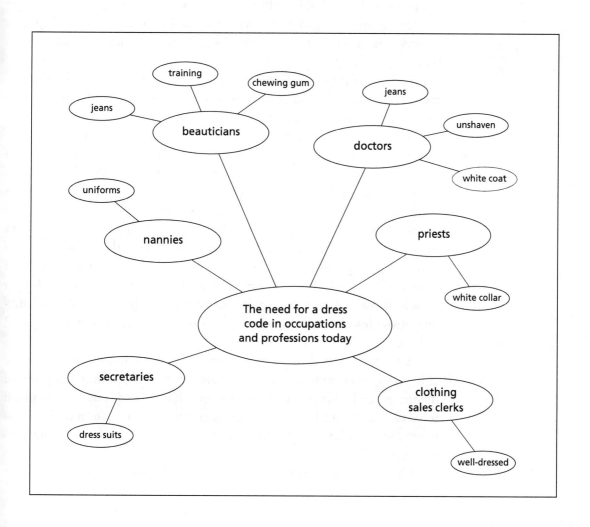

This diagram illustrates one way to make some sense of the many possible relationships among the ideas that might be discussed in the writing in chapter 1 on the need for a dress code in various occupations and professions today. The writer has placed the topic in the center of the collected ideas, then drawn lines to indicate connections to satellites that identify six professions in which individuals once wore a uniform or specific type of clothing to distinguish their occupation or profession: doctors, priests, beauticians, nannies, secretaries, clothing store salesclerks. Two of the satellite ideas, beauticians and doctors, become the centers of their own limited clusters. These minor clusters should provide the writer with more support ideas for the writing, while the remaining four satellites will probably offer fewer ideas to develop. Using the clustering method allows the writer to highlight the relationships between ideas and to more easily discard any that are not worth exploring.

Another method of sorting and categorizing to highlight the relationships among ideas is *branching,* a technique similar to clustering. A range of supporting ideas "branch out" from the main writing topic; the writer lists these below the main topic in no specific order. In making the initial branching list, the writer leaves substantial space between each major idea to allow for the development of minor ideas and their connection to the major branches. Each main idea will develop into a section of the writing, and each smaller branch or specific idea will be used to support the main idea to which it is connected. Although very carefully organized, the branching diagram is not an outline, because it only lists major and minor ideas and shows their relationships, but not the order in which those relationships will be discussed. In contrast, an outline provides the specific order of the ideas that the writing will follow.

A writer is asked to provide a review of local public records, such as licenses and permits, property-related transactions, public reports of meetings and filings, and annual municipal and county financial reports, that might be made available to reporters to use in their newspaper stories. How might the material be organized using the branching method?

The branch diagram for this topic should look like this:

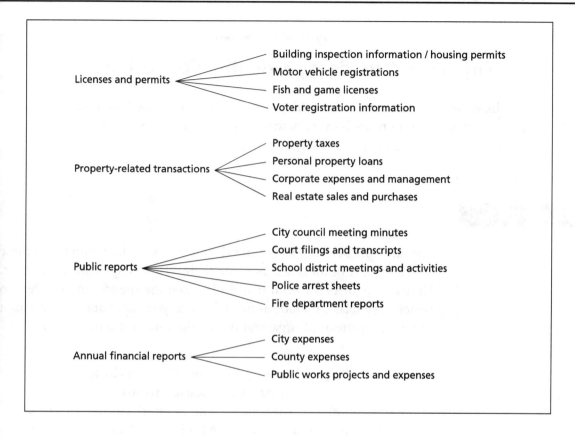

This organization of ideas is only one of many ways of categorization that a writer might use to develop an essay or article that reveals the extensive information available through local public records. Some writers might choose to create categories for private versus public activities, or might separate the ideas along financial and civic lines. The major divisions can be increased or decreased and additional minor ideas might be added to support a larger number of major idea categories. Even if a writer chooses to keep the present branching divisions, the order might be modified as the actual writing (or records, in the example) demands a greater emphasis upon one area above others. However the material might be reorganized, the branching process will remain beneficial to the final writing process, for it allows the writer to establish meaningful connections among the many ideas available.

---

┌─────────────────────────────────────────────────┐
│ ▭▭▷ QUICK TIP ▭▭▶

# Organize Your Ideas to Identify Connections

Use either the clustering or branching approach to determine how your
support ideas relate to each other before you begin to write.
└─────────────────────────────────────────────────┘

**SELF-TEST**

For the topic below, select either the clustering or branching technique
to create a list of ideas and indicate their relationships with each other.
Create categories for both major ideas and the specific minor ideas to
which they relate. Include as many ideas as you can, but do not attempt
to create a pattern of organization for the final writing.

### Topic: Making Teachers Take Periodic Competency Examinations

A large number of ideas may come to mind, because this topic
has been under public debate on both the federal and local levels. Those in favor offer numerous reasons why testing teachers
periodically is good for education, while the opposition is
equally vehement in listing and backing what it views as the
negative aspects of the issue. Can you take a clear position either
for or against the testing? If so, focus your clustering of ideas or
branching on either completely supporting the issue or completely denying its validity. If you do not see the argument of
either side as fully valid, then devise a cluster of ideas or branching to reflect this inability to commit yourself to one side or to
the other.

**ANSWER**

Which technique have you chosen? For this exercise, we have used the
branching technique, although clustering would work just as well.

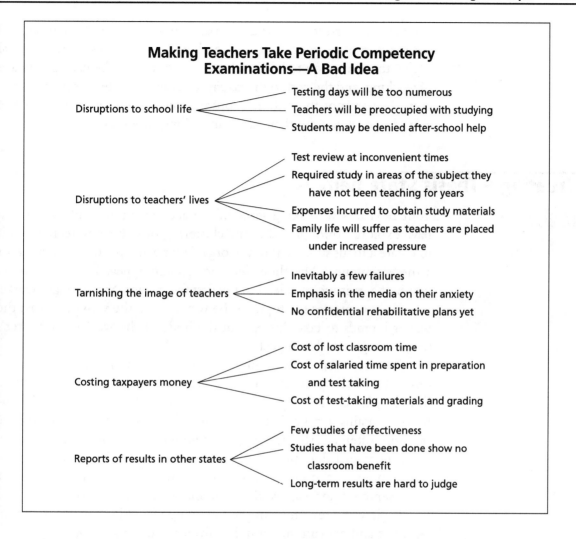

## Making Teachers Take Periodic Competency Examinations—A Bad Idea

Disruptions to school life
- Testing days will be too numerous
- Teachers will be preoccupied with studying
- Students may be denied after-school help

Disruptions to teachers' lives
- Test review at inconvenient times
- Required study in areas of the subject they have not been teaching for years
- Expenses incurred to obtain study materials
- Family life will suffer as teachers are placed under increased pressure

Tarnishing the image of teachers
- Inevitably a few failures
- Emphasis in the media on their anxiety
- No confidential rehabilitative plans yet

Costing taxpayers money
- Cost of lost classroom time
- Cost of salaried time spent in preparation and test taking
- Cost of test-taking materials and grading

Reports of results in other states
- Few studies of effectiveness
- Studies that have been done show no classroom benefit
- Long-term results are hard to judge

The topic did not take a position, but the writer must take a position and make that viewpoint clear at the outset of the writing. To keep the focus of the writing clearly in mind, the main topic (the title in the above) should express that position. In the branching diagrams above, some of the minor ideas may fit into more than one category, but you must restrict your choice to the category that is related most strongly to the idea. The order of the ideas is not as important, because you will later move around the various related categories and find that you have completed much of the thinking toward developing those thoughts while planning the clustering or branching exercise. The relationships identified in the diagram show great promise as the basis for an essay on the subject, and the opposition to the plan to test teachers may be attacked from several angles: the disruption to life (teachers' and students'), the damaged image of teaching, and the cost to the taxpayer. As appropriate as they are, however, they are not the only relationships and the writer should not feel bound to dealing with them alone in writing about the topic.

## Creating a Thesis Statement

Your next task in making sense of the accumulation of ideas that you have explored through either the clustering or branching techniques is to create a focus statement of the organizing principle of the writing, or a thesis sentence. The thesis sentence should appear in the first paragraph of a writing, or at least in the first few paragraphs in longer works, because it expresses the topic of the writing and the viewpoint that the writer intends to take throughout the body of the work—the writer's specific angle on the subject.

The thesis sentence is more of a risk to the writer than the previously discussed approaches to organizing ideas. Rather than simply a listing of ideas and their relationships with each other, the thesis sentence contains a central idea that includes a definite and identifiable opinion, often clearly indicated by the use of a specific word or phrase. A sentence that does not express a conviction—the bolder the conviction expressed, the better and more interesting the writing—is not a thesis sentence and has less of a unifying effect on the writing.

Review the sentences in the following example. Identify the thesis sentence and explain how it differs from the other sentence.

Sentence 1    The state plans to require that all teachers take tests of competence in their subject areas every five years.

Sentence 2    The state should require that all teachers in the public schools take tests of competence in their subject areas every five years and continue to take courses as long as they teach.

Sentence 1 identifies the topic and relates a fact related to the plans of the state in regard to testing teachers, but it does not take a stand or express an opinion. The reader can expect that the writing to follow will contain similar facts and information, but the sentence does not express a controlling idea or key word to reveal a specific direction or to limit its focus.

Sentence 2 identifies the topic and expresses a definite strong opinion about the issue. The generalization expressed in this sentence signals readers to be alert and to watch for the supporting details to follow in the body of the writing. Think of the thesis sentence as a signpost, leading to the specific thoughts of the writer. If the writer follows the organizing principle of the thesis, then both the writer and the reader will reach the same final destination—in this case, clear communication regarding a given topic. On the other hand, if the writer ignores the organizing principle and chooses to write about ideas and concepts that are not promised by the thesis, the reader will be lost. In short, the writer will have failed in the task of trying to communicate with the reader.

Write a thesis sentence for each of the following topics:

1. pets in apartments

2. cell phone use while driving

3. safety of airline passengers

Thesis sentences that might be written to express ideas about topic 1 are numerous, even if the topic appears to be rather benign or limited in scope. In contrast, topics 2 and 3 appear to be more limited in scope, but this perception is inaccurate. Both offer the possibility of numerous approaches, which depend on the goals of the writer and the needs of the readers.

Below are three thesis sentences for each of the three topics. Each sentence grows out of a different combination or subset of supporting ideas and represents a different central idea or organizing principle for the topic. Read each sentence carefully to see how the use of key words or phrases creates a different focus.

1. Pets in apartments

    a. The close proximity of many apartments can make keeping a pet in an apartment dangerous to the health of others in surrounding apartments. [*From the perspective of others living in the apartment building or complex*]

b.  Apartment dwellers should not own large dogs, because confining such animals who require freedom to run and to enjoy frequent exercise is an act of cruelty. [*From the perspective of one category of pets*]

c.  Landlords and building superintendents should not be permitted to deny renters the right to have pets. [*From the perspective of potential pet owners*]

2.  Cell phone use while driving

a.  The new law that will ban people from talking on cell phones while driving is another form of unwelcome government intrusion and represents harassment of respectable citizens. [*From the perspective of a cell phone owner who vehemently opposes the ban*]

b.  Too many lives have been lost needlessly in accidents that occurred while the guilty party was talking on a cell phone, and states should ban the practice. [*From the perspective of either law enforcement or other parties who agree with the ban*]

c.  Driving long distances can be boring and the monotony often causes drivers to fall asleep at the wheel, but talking on a cell phone can be life-saving because doing so keeps the driver alert and responsive. [*From the perspective of a cell phone owner who opposes the ban in certain circumstances*]

3.  Airline passenger safety

a.  Increased checkpoints and greater security on board airplanes are needed to make airline passengers confident that air travel is safe. [*From the perspective of a transportation safety analyst or an observer of existing airline procedures*]

b.  Flying makes many people nervous, but increased delays at airports, longer waits at check-in locations, and new security measures at the gates are inconveniences that serve to distract and decrease the nervousness of many. [*From the perspective of an airline passenger*]

---

┌─────────────────────────────────────────────────────┐

◻══════◻ **QUICK TIP** ■═══════►

# Reveal Your Angle on the Topic at the Outset

Include in your opening paragraph a thesis statement that contains the controlling idea of the writing and that reveals your angle on the topic.

└─────────────────────────────────────────────────────┘

    c.  Passenger safety is foremost in the minds of many airline executives, but the costs of assuring such safety are more than a smaller company such as ours can afford. [*From the perspective of an airline decision maker*]

**SELF-TEST**

Read the following sentences carefully and decide which are simply statements, and which meet the requirements of a thesis sentence. Remember that a thesis sentence must express a viewpoint about a topic and provide a logical direction for the writing.

1. The recipe requires fresh ingredients from your garden.

2. Fresh fruits and vegetables provide health benefits that cannot be found in over-the-counter vitamins.

3. The library contains many newspapers and magazines that may be read in the building, but they cannot be taken out.

4. The new television programs provide a variety of police procedural programs, situation comedies, and musical variety shows.

5. The city Little League baseball field is dangerous for our children to play on and must be renovated before the new season begins.

6. Seven of the ten players on the winning college basketball team played in YMCA intramural programs.

7. Leadership qualities develop early in children who are involved in team sports.

8. The school board vetoed the creation of eight new courses last year.

9. Tom Brokaw has given the label "the Greatest Generation" to people who lived through the Great Depression and World War II.

10. Citizens in a town should have the right to determine what their children read in school and should have veto power over which books are purchased by the public library.

## ANSWERS

1. Statement of fact that offers information but no angle or viewpoint on the topic. With the addition of the writer's opinion or viewpoint, this could easily become a strong thesis statement.

2. Thesis statement because it provides an organizing principle for a writing that will include supporting ideas to exhibit the health benefits of specific fruits and vegetables.

3. Statement of fact that offers information but no angle or viewpoint on the topic. With the addition of the writer's opinion or viewpoint, this could easily become a strong thesis statement.

4. Statement of fact that offers information but no angle or viewpoint on the topic. With the addition of the writer's opinion or viewpoint, this could easily become a strong thesis statement.

5. Thesis statement because it contains a strongly worded opinion of the condition of a Little League baseball field. The statement labels the field "dangerous" and asserts that work must be completed to improve it. The writer's supporting details must identify the specific dangers and provide solutions to the problem.

6. Statement of fact that offers information but no angle or viewpoint on the topic. With the addition of the writer's opinion or viewpoint, this could easily become a strong thesis statement.

7. Thesis statement that probably appears at the beginning of a lengthy writing and will likely be further refined by the addition of several sentences (subthesis sentences) in the first few paragraphs of the piece. The writer must more clearly define the focus for an effective effort.

8. Statement of fact that offers information but no angle or viewpoint on the topic. With the addition of the writer's opinion or viewpoint, this could easily become a strong thesis statement.

9. Statement of fact that offers information but no angle or viewpoint on the topic. With the addition of the writer's opinion or viewpoint, this could easily become a strong thesis statement.

10. Thesis statement that provides a strong statement of viewpoint, but fails to include the reasons why citizens should be allowed such power. As with 7, the writer will most likely follow this statement with several clarifying statements to inform readers why the stand is necessary.

# Organizing Information

Writing clearly does not always require a rigid outline, but you do have to decide how the material is to be organized: chronologically, spatially, or logically. For some topics, the use of clustering or branching suggests ways the writing can be most effectively organized, and several choices exist. For other topics, however, the information can be presented in only one order, and forcing the supporting details into any other order will make the writer's point incoherent.

In **chronological order,** the writer presents ideas and specific details in time sequence, in the order they occurred. This approach works best if actual events are discussed or used to support the viewpoint expressed in the thesis sentence.

In **spatial order,** the writer presents ideas and specific details organized geographically or otherwise related to physical content. This approach works best if the writing uses descriptions of physical sites or scenes.

In **logical order,** the writer presents ideas and specific details organized to focus attention on the most important ideas. In this approach, the writer places the most important idea or point either at the beginning or the end of the writing. To do this requires that the writing begin with the most important idea and place less important ideas afterward, or begin with less important ideas and build up to the idea to which the reader should pay the most attention.

Read each of the following thesis sentences. Determine which order the writer should use to develop the topic and viewpoint expressed: chronological, spatial, or logical.

1.  Fresh fruits and vegetables provide health benefits that cannot be found in over-the-counter vitamins.

2.  The city Little League baseball field is dangerous for our children to play on and must be renovated before the new season begins.

3.  Leadership qualities develop early in children who are involved in team sports.

Thesis sentence 1 will benefit most from a *logical* ordering of ideas and supporting details, and the writer might build the argument for the reader by beginning with the least important benefit of fresh fruits and vegetables and moving to the most important benefit. The discussion of each benefit should contain supporting discussion of the vitamin content and may also include discussion of fiber content, solubility, and other health-related issues.

Thesis sentence 2 requires a *spatial* ordering of ideas, which will allow the writer to methodically examine those areas of the field that pose dangers to the children and to provide details of places in which renovations can be made. The choice of supporting details will be guided by the physical layout of the field, to provide an organized approach to those features that require attention and those that do not.

Thesis sentence 3 will best be developed if *chronological* order is used. The supporting details should be selected to reflect the growth of lead-

---

╒═══════╕ QUICK TIP ▬▬▶

# Organize Carefully

Before you write, decide which order to use in presenting ideas: chronological, spatial, or logical. Allow the topic to determine the most effective order.

---

ership skills and qualities as they change and increase with the month-to-month increase in the ages of children involved in different team sports.

**SELF-TEST**

Review carefully each of the thesis sentences below and decide the order the writer must use to create the most effective expression of the topic and viewpoint. If more than one order seems possible, select the one that you believe would be the most effective.

1. Children thrive in households that place emphasis upon family togetherness and respect for each member's needs.

2. Teachers should be given periodic retraining and access to continuing education courses over their entire careers.

3. With its many small neighborhoods, Passaic, New Jersey, has always been a center of cultural diversity.

4. Once the national pastime, baseball has now become only one of several sports that capture the national interest.

5. Few baseball parks can compete in historical value with Yankee Stadium.

6. The United States must change its immigration policies, after the tragic attack on the World Trade Center on September 11, 2001.

7. Children whose parents read to them are better prepared for class and have stronger communication skills than their classmates whose parents do not read to them.

8. Very few buildings can compare to the Empire State Building as a source of architectural interest.

### ANSWERS

1. Logical order.   The supporting details will consist of examples of family togetherness and mutual respect, presented in order from least important to most important.

2. Chronological order.   The supporting details will identify various career stages in teaching and pinpoint the types of retraining and education that would be appropriate at each stage.

3. Spatial order.   The supporting details will identify neighborhoods that are examples of the cultural diversity of the city and present a neighborhood-by-neighborhood analysis.

4. Chronological order.   The supporting details will identify changing perceptions of baseball over time and compare its popularity in different times to its popularity today.

5. Chronological order.   The supporting details will identify historical high points in stadium history from its earliest days to the present. (The thesis could also be developed using spatial order, if the writer decides to use stadium landmarks as examples to discuss historical value.)

6. Logical order.   The supporting details will discuss the less important reasons for limiting immigration, related to the attacks, and build up to the most important reason.

7. Logical order.   The supporting details will discuss the preparation and communication skills needed for classroom success, in order of importance from least to most, and relate the importance of each to reading.

8. Spatial order.   The supporting details will methodically identify notable architectural details of the Empire State Building and discuss their unique nature.

## Finding and Writing Your Topic

1. Ask the questions about the topic that you, and your reader, want the writing to answer.
2. Use clustering or branching to identify the relationships among support ideas.
3. Create a thesis sentence that reveals your angle on the topic at the outset.
4. Select the most appropriate order of organization for your topic.

**CHAPTER SELF-TEST**

Read the following list of sentences and identify the thesis statements by placing a "T" on the line preceding each item. Place an "N" on the line preceding each sentence that is not a thesis sentence. For each thesis sentence that you identify, underline the most appropriate order of organization for the details that will be used as support in the writing.

1. _____ The history of ancient Egypt contains stories of numerous animal gods and goddesses that ruled the daily lives of the ancient Egyptians. (chronological    spatial    logical)

2. _____ Soldiers who fought in the Vietnam War have been wrongfully denied the respect given to soldiers who have fought in other U.S. wars. (chronological    spatial    logical)

3. _____ The city of Paterson, New Jersey, designed by Alexander Hamilton, reflects geographically his sense of order and symmetry. (chronological    spatial    logical)

4. _____ Censors must learn to understand what playwright Oscar Wilde once wrote: "There are no bad books, only books that are badly written."
(chronological    spatial    logical)

5. _____ Intelligence develops continuously, increasing yearly until the individual reaches the age of fourteen.
(chronological    spatial    logical)

6. ____ Most people become more understanding and tolerant of the failings of others as they grow older and suffer greater adversity. (chronological    spatial    logical)

7. ____ The average age of a first marriage in this state is eighteen years. (chronological    spatial    logical)

8. ____ Filmmaking should be considered an art, comparable in importance to sculpture and painting.
(chronological    spatial    logical)

9. ____ Hotels in various parts of the nation have successfully lured guests to their sites by using clever salesmanship and generous promotions. (chronological    spatial    logical)

10. ____ College students begin to learn to appreciate their hometowns and family life more as they become older.
(chronological    spatial    logical)

**ANSWERS**

1.  _N_
2.  _T_   logical
3.  _T_   spatial
4.  _T_   logical
5.  _T_   chronological
6.  _T_   chronological
7.  _N_
8.  _T_   logical
9.  _T_   spatial
10. _T_   chronological

# 3 Writing a Strong Introduction

## Objectives

In this chapter you will learn to:

- determine how much or how little information to reveal in the introduction

- select an appropriate opening for your topic (anecdotal, factual, or question)

- make the transition to the body of the writing

A good introduction is as important to writing as a good first impression is in professional and social interactions. Introduce your writing with as much effort and attention to detail as you would take to make a good first impression. Once readers are attracted by your opening lines, they will be more likely to keep reading and to consider seriously the ideas and arguments that follow.

Newswriters and other professionals polish their introductory paragraphs to hook readers and keep them reading—or risk losing an audience and markets for their future writings. Approach your writing in the same way, even if most of your readers are a captive audience—teachers, friends, coworkers. Capture the interest and attention of your readers at the outset and your writing will communicate your message more clearly and with greater impact.

Do not make the mistake of believing the body of the text is so compelling that it eliminates the need for a carefully written introduction. However interesting and vital the information, you still owe readers at the outset a clear statement of the topic, your angle on the topic, and a generalization of the supporting details you will use to back up your views. Take the time to craft an effective introductory paragraph (or paragraphs, in longer writings) to capture reader interest at the outset, or risk being misunderstood or ignored.

# Choosing How Much to Reveal in the Introduction

The introduction paragraph is a personal sales pitch that should interest, seduce, and lure your readers into reading the rest of the writing, while also giving them a clear idea of what will follow. Provide too much information and readers become overwhelmed, stop, and never make it to the body text. Provide too little information and readers will interpret this as indifference to the topic and stop reading.

Length is another concern, although word count is not always an accurate measure of the value of the ideas within the paragraph. Writing made up of many sentences containing only generalizations and repetition may actually provide very little information, while brief paragraphs may contain an abundance of ideas. Nonetheless, keep the word count of the introduction to a reasonable length, from 50 to 150 words, to inform readers and pique their interest without burdening them.

The only way to assure that your writing will be read is to strike the right balance, and to present your information in a direct manner with clarity, passion, and imagination. Give your reader something to look forward to—not to dread. A good opening paragraph states the writer's case clearly and sets the pace for the rest of the writing. If you do not work at the outset to ignite the reader's interest, why bother to write the rest of the piece?

Think like a reader when you write an introduction. When you read, you want to know what to expect before spending valuable minutes poring over an article, letter, or essay—and so do your readers.

Take a direct approach and keep the following guidelines in mind when writing an introduction:

1. Be considerate of your readers and realize that their time is valuable.

2. Formulate a clear, strongly worded thesis sentence and reveal your viewpoint in the first or last sentence of the introduction.

3. Write for a well-informed reader—a particular audience—unless told to do otherwise.

4. Avoid attempting to include all facets of a topic, but provide a good overview.

5. Do not bombard readers with vague statements and generalizations if you really have nothing of substance to write about a topic.

6. Either choose a topic about which you can write with authority—and exhibit that authority in the introduction—or do the research necessary to acquire the necessary understanding and expertise.

7. List specific details and support ideas that will appear in the body text and review them mentally as you write the introduction.

8. Skip the temptation to dazzle your readers in the introduction with fancy prose and trick phrases, especially when what follows lacks substance and interest.

9. Save the specific details for development in the body of the writing, but do reveal enough in the introduction to inform the reader fully about the writing's purpose.

10. Make certain that the introduction promises only what the writing will deliver.

As you read the following examples, decide whether each writer succeeds or fails in making an effective opening pitch. Consider what you would have written if asked to complete the same assignment. Would your opening paragraph look like one of the three below? If not, how would it differ? Why?

The three examples below were written as introductions for the following essay assignment:

> The United States has long been viewed as the land of opportunity for immigrants from many nations who come to U.S. shores expecting to find a nation ready to welcome them and to help them succeed. This has been called "the American Dream." Write an essay in which you discuss and evaluate the concept of "the American Dream." Support your views with specific examples from what you have read, heard, viewed, and experienced regarding the topic.

Which of the following opening paragraphs would make you keep reading? Why is it more successful than the other two? Where might the writers of the other two paragraphs make changes to successfully capture the intention of the assignment?

## Example 1

People complain that the United States is no longer the land of opportunity. Many point to the squalor and poverty in which immigrants to both the big cities and the border towns live, but they fail to look at the many who have also become successful pursuing their version of the American Dream. I also have many examples from my past and from my family life that prove them wrong. (71 words)

## Example 2

The American Dream is dead for many immigrants who came to the United States in the last half of the twentieth century, because the old dream of the U.S. as a "land of opportunity" has turned into a nightmare. Jobs are scarce for people who have limited English-speaking capabilities, credentials proving their professional training in their homelands are not respected, and potential employers find ways to demean them as early as the interview process. Social service programs make promises to help legal immigrants, but few of those promises result in good jobs, safe housing, and adequate medical care for immigrant families. Signs may be posted in various towns to state that Spanish (or Polish, Korean, Hindi, or other languages) is spoken in the public offices or is present in bilingual programs in the schools, but help is not available to turn the promises of those signs into opportunities for success. Recent immigrants learn that there is nowhere to turn and no one to care when they need assistance. New restrictions on immigration and on legal immigrants will now make opportunities in the U.S. even scarcer, as the federal government places limits on the amount and type of aid for which immigrant families will be eligible. Instead of the land of opportunity, the U.S. has become the land of frustration, humiliation, and poverty for the many immigrants who are lured here by what have now become false promises. (237 words)

### Example 3

My parents were Polish immigrants who came to this great country of ours with nothing more than a few dollars in their pockets. They found jobs in factories and endured the low pay and difficult conditions in order to achieve their goals. Not only did they live on their earnings, but they also saved money to send back to Poland to support their families. Many immigrant families today are doing this and more to make "the American Dream" work for them. (83 words)

In these examples, the length of the passage has no relationship to the quality of the information provided. For example, passages 1 and 3, while of similar length, are not similarly effective, and, at 237 words, passage 2 is less effective in providing information than the other two, despite being three times as long. Word count alone does not determine the quality of an introduction.

Let's reconsider the three examples and assess how successful they are as introduction paragraphs.

### Example 1

People complain that the United States is no longer the land of opportunity. Many point to the squalor and poverty in which immigrants to both the big cities and the border towns live, but they fail to look at the many who have also become successful pursuing their version of the American Dream. [*The writer must provide a transition at this point to link the generalization regarding the*

*American Dream and the general reference to the writer's examples from the past and from family. The writer must also identify several of those "many examples" from the past and "from my family" for a strong thesis sentence.*] I also have many examples from my past [*identify several*] and from my family life [*identify several*] that prove them wrong. [*The paragraph offers too little information and the included thesis sentence is weak.*]

## Example 2

The American Dream is dead for many immigrants who came to the United States in the last half of the twentieth century, because the old dream of the U.S. as a "land of opportunity" has turned into a nightmare. Jobs are scarce for people who have limited English-speaking capabilities, credentials proving their professional training in their homelands are not respected, and employers find ways to demean them as early as the interview process. Social service programs make promises to help legal immigrants, but few of those promises result in good jobs, safe housing, and adequate medical care for immigrant families. Signs may be posted in various towns to state that Spanish (or Polish, Korean, Hindi, or other languages) is spoken in the public offices or is present in bilingual programs in the schools, but help is not available to turn the promises of those signs into opportunities for success. Recent immigrants learn that there is nowhere to turn and no one to care when they need assistance. New restrictions on immigration and on legal immigrants will now make opportunities in the U.S. even scarcer, as the federal government places limits on the amount and type of aid for which immigrant families will be eligible. Instead of the land of opportunity, the U.S. has become the land of frustration, humiliation, and poverty for the many immigrants who are lured here by what have now become false promises. [*The overlong introduction paragraph bombards the reader with specific information from the outset of the writing, but the controlling idea phrased in the thesis sentence does not appear until the final statement. Therefore the reader must plod through numerous specific details that properly belong in the body text before learning of the guiding principle or intention of the writing. The numerous details are also too vast in scope, and they overwhelm the thesis statement that appears at the end of the overly lengthy paragraph.*]

---

╓═══╕ QUICK TIP ◄█████►

# Reveal Only What You Must in the Introduction

Do not give the reader too much or too little information. Aim to intrigue readers and entice them to read on through your writing.

---

### Example 3

My parents were Polish immigrants who came to this great country of ours with nothing more than a few dollars in their pockets. They found jobs in factories and endured the low pay and difficult conditions in order to achieve their goals. Not only did they live on their earnings, but they also saved money to send back to Poland to support their families. *Many immigrant families today are making the same sacrifices and more to make "the American Dream" work for them.* [*The paragraph provides an anecdote to begin the writing, then segues into a thesis sentence (set here in italics) that links the past to contemporary immigrant families who reflect the same hopes, dreams, and values as those of the writer's parents. The thesis sentence also suggests that the American Dream can still provide immigrant families with the successes found in the past, if they follow the example set by the writer's parents and other immigrants.*]

**SELF-TEST**

Read carefully the following topic statement and the introduction paragraph written to examine the issue. The sentences are numbered to assist our discussion. Assess the relevance of the introduction to the assigned topic, giving attention to both the thesis sentence and the context set by the opening sentences. Decide what changes are needed to make this a strong introduction paragraph. Rewrite the paragraph to include changes that you would make, such as modifying or omitting sentences that detract from paragraph unity, adding sentences, and creating a thesis sentence that clearly indicates the intentions for the writing. As you rewrite and edit the paragraph, keep in mind the principles reviewed earlier in this chapter on creating the well-written introduction.

**Topic: Cultural Diversity**

(1) People today speak about cultural diversity as if it were a new idea, but many years ago, I grew up in a neighborhood that contained a broad range of nationalities and cultures. (2) Educators talk about the need for different ethnic groups to learn about each other's customs and beliefs. (3) Politicians make references to their platforms for underrepresented parts of the population. (4) Church and civic leaders call for people of all colors and national backgrounds to join in a common cause. (5) The news media make a major point of focusing attention on events that are cosponsored by organizations representing different cultures or people of different ethnic backgrounds. (6) Poor neighborhoods contain a mix of people from different nations and different cultural backgrounds. (7) People learn that they have to work together when they live with each other in close quarters.

**ANSWER**

The paragraph presents several difficulties, ranging from inconsistencies in expression to a lack of a defined thesis sentence. Although it opens with a statement that suggests a personal perspective will be expressed in the writing, the sentences that follow contradict that perspective as broader examples are offered and draw attention away from the more interesting, seemingly more personal account that was first promised. The writer must make a decision as to the focus of the writing, then make the necessary revisions to produce an introduction paragraph that incorporates that focus. Whether the writer chooses to use a personal or a global context in the introduction, the writing can, in both cases, draw supporting details from personal experiences in regard to cultural diversity.

Setting the thesis in a personal context, sentences 1, 6, and 7 from the original paragraph should be kept, modified, and incorporated into an expanded introduction that omits the remaining sentences, 2, 3, 4, and 5. The writer must also develop a thesis sentence that incorporates the personal perspective and indicates the direction that the writing will follow. Below is one way in which this might be accomplished.

People today speak about cultural diversity as if it were a new idea, but it is not. Those who grew up in poor neighborhoods, as I did, become familiar with a broad range of nationalities and cultures. My neighbors were a mix of people from different nations and different cultural backgrounds. Rather than having to be told by politicians and other leaders that we had to get along, we knew from experience that people who live together in close quarters have to work with one another.

The writer may also provide a global context for the topic of cultural diversity, using sentences 2, 3, 4, and 5 to provide the broader context. The writer's personal experiences can be used to provide the supporting discussion of the writing, and the thesis sentence expresses the personal perspective that follows the generalizations in the first part of the introduction paragraph.

Educators talk about the need for different ethnic groups to learn about each other's customs and beliefs. Politicians make references to their platforms for underrepresented parts of the population. Church and civic leaders call for people of all colors and national backgrounds to join in a common cause. The news media make a major point of focusing attention on events that are cosponsored by organizations representing different cultures or people of different ethnic backgrounds. All of this attention is important in illuminating the issue, but it is not the best way to bring people together. Living in a culturally diverse neighborhood as a child, I learned that harmony among different cultures is best achieved when people of diverse backgrounds live near each other and share common experiences.

# Selecting an Appropriate Opening

The introduction paragraph has a weighty task to perform. It must capture the attention of readers and introduce accurately the key points of the writing to follow, while maintaining readers' interest. The writer can use a variety of techniques to begin the introduction, but the most workable approaches are the anecdotal, factual, and question beginnings.

The **anecdotal approach**'s introduction begins with a brief story the writer uses as an example to lead into the larger concern of the writing. The anecdote must be chosen carefully so that it reflects the thesis sentence, as well as the larger point expressed throughout the body of the writing. The danger for many inexperienced writers who use the anecdotal opening is that readers do not always understand as clearly as the writer the connection between the brief story and the larger discussion. At best, the reader is forced to ignore the anecdotal opening and is left to simply concentrate on the thesis sentence and supporting discussion. At worst, the badly chosen anecdote will bewilder the reader, who will stop reading after the thesis sentence. Read the following example and see how the anecdote chosen by the writer sets a context for the thesis sentence that completes the introduction.

> The nurse's voice seemed to echo when she called my name. I stood up, hoisted my bulging purse to my shoulder, and marched resolutely out of the waiting room behind her. The sharp shoulder and back pains that had kept me awake for nearly a month pulsed, and the fear that I had a serious illness returned. Once in the examining room, I told the doctor of the pain, and he prepared to examine me. He winced as he lifted my purse off the stool. In a moment, we both reached the same diagnosis— my overfilled purse, not a life-threatening illness, was the source of my pain. This incident happened twenty years ago and taught me a lesson. Many fears are baseless and can be eliminated, if we approach them in a rational manner.

The writer offers an anecdote about a commonplace experience to initiate a discussion of baseless fears and how to deal with them. The reader is caught up in the brief drama of the writer's fear that the pain may be the sign of a serious injury or illness, then realizes the irony of the reason behind the pain. In order to provide an indication that her realization regarding fear has been tested since the incident, the writer establishes a time frame in the sentence preceding the thesis sentence, to inform readers that enough time has passed to permit additional fear-related situations to have occurred and the results to have confirmed her observation. The paragraph culminates in the summation—thesis sentence—suggesting that a range of similar fear-related situations will be examined in the body text and confirming the realization that rational analysis can eliminate many such fears.

Using the **factual approach** in the introduction is a second effective way to begin a piece of writing, and it is especially successful when responding to an essay question on an examination, writing an analysis or report, or drafting an editorial, although other types of writing can also benefit from the technique. In an introduction using the factual approach, the writer first offers readers a series of facts—statements that can be proved or disproved—and provides a thesis sentence that sums them up and either supports their validity or suggests that they are erroneous. The wise writer chooses the facts carefully, so that they create a desired effect in the reader. Review the example below and assess the writer's selection of facts. Consider how the same set of facts might result in different thesis sentences and, as a result, a different direction for the writing.

> Forty-three students failed the state Test of Basic English Skills, while sixty-three students failed the state Test of Basic Math Skills. College entrance test scores hover consistently around the twentieth percentile, and only 10 percent of graduates attend four-year colleges. The student dropout rate for the last five years averages 15 percent. The dismal student performance levels of XYZ High School must be reversed, and only a state takeover of the school district can improve conditions.

This brief paragraph contains clearly stated statistics that cast the subject high school in an unfavorable light, a judgment most people would agree with. The facts report the low test scores, high dropout rate, and low college attendance levels of the high school, which may lead to a range of possible discussions. The writer first comments on the negative information, then provides one suggested direction that might be taken to reverse the trend. Other writers might have other suggestions for improving the situation. Still another approach to the facts might be to downplay their importance in light of greater problems that can be identified, or to use them to illustrate existing additional problems in the school district.

A third effective way to begin an introduction is the **question approach,** first posing a series of questions to the reader, then providing a thesis sentence that answers the questions either by agreeing with their implications or by refuting them. The questions are usually rhetorical, and the writer does not expect the specific questions to receive answers. Instead, readers proceeding from one question to another build up emotional or intellectual responses that are met with the writer's actual point, expressed in the thesis sentence. Politicians use this technique in drawing voters to their points of view, professors use the question approach as a classroom technique to elicit student responses, and writers of propaganda find that leaving carefully crafted and ordered questions unanswered is effective in swaying thinking to their viewpoints. In some cases, the writer poses only one comprehensive question, then provides a generalized response before stating the specific thesis sentence. Read the following introduction paragraph and analyze the writer's use of questions to introduce the thesis sentence.

> How long will this war continue? Why are we putting our servicemen and -women in harm's way for another nation? When will we be able to lift this terrible sadness from our hearts? Seeing those we love go to war is never easy, but, in this case, the pain is deeper because many of us know in our hearts that we are fighting in an unjust cause.

The questions are posed in a specific order that is designed to evoke an emotional response from the reader, and the writer finishes with an emotionally charged thesis sentence that would appear too abrupt if presented on its own. The rhetorical questions prepare the reader, paving the way for the writer's point of view and making it more acceptable as it directly follows the rhetorical questions. Carefully crafted though it is, such a response to the questions might not be the choice of another writer. Using the same questions as a lead-in to the thesis sentence, other points might be made regarding the effect of war on nations and individuals, the policies of the specific nation's government, the efforts of groups to end the war, or a range of issues related to the motivations behind the war.

---

**◁▭▭ QUICK TIP ▭▭▷**

## Select an Opening Tailored for Your Topic

Lead your reader to the ideas expressed in the thesis statement by using the anecdotal, factual, or question approach. The gradual approach will increase their understanding.

**SELF-TEST**

Consider all aspects of the following topic and create three different intro-duction paragraphs, using each of the three main approaches for writing opening paragraphs: anecdotal, factual, and question. Make certain that the details you provide to create the context for the thesis sentence are accurate. You may have to create three different thesis sentences as well.

### Topic: Athletics or Academics?

## Anecdotal Approach

_____

_____

_____

## Factual Approach

_____

_____

_____

## Question Approach

_____

_____

_____

**ANSWERS**

Compare your answers with the versions that appear below. The topic is broad enough to permit the development of numerous issues and a seemingly limitless number of ways in which to examine each issue.

## Anecdotal Approach

The grocery bagger packed the last item and lowered it into my cart, then smiled and pleasantly wished me a good day. After returning his smile, I offered my thanks and walked toward the door, my mind racing to remember the young man's name. I had never taught him in class, but I remembered his face. A decade ago, he had been the star of every football pep rally for three of his four high school years. His coach had bullied teachers and lobbied administrators to make certain that his star player would not be benched for a game, but he never asked how his player was doing in class. From his current job, I guessed that college must not have worked out, nor did he have the predicted professional football career. High schools must stop victimizing student athletes and should give as much attention to their academic preparation as to their preparation in sports.

## Factual Approach

Only 23 percent of students entering X University on athletic scholarships graduate in less than six years. Nearly 48 percent of these students take six or more years to graduate. Twenty-nine percent of students entering on athletic scholarships never finish their degrees. These figures contrast greatly with those of students entering either on academic or need-based scholarships or with no financial aid at all. Seventy-eight percent of all nonathletes graduate in six years or less, only 6 percent take more than six years to complete their degrees, and just 16 percent leave without earning their degrees. The administration must take these differences seriously, identify the reasons for the lower academic performance of student athletes, and devise a program that will elevate the levels of academic achievement among student athletes at X University.

## Question Approach

Why is so much money being spent on upgrading the sports arena? Is paying laundry costs and supplying free housing to student athletes legal? Must the development of new classroom and laboratory facilities always take a backseat to spending for new sports equipment? Can the university justify offering student athletes twice the number of scholarship dollars that it offers nonathlete incoming students? The time has come for us to reevaluate our priorities and to provide our academic students with the same opportunities given to student athletes.

# Making the Transition from the Introduction to the Body Paragraphs

The transition from the introduction to the body paragraphs is the responsibility of the thesis sentence, which, when structured correctly, should provide you with an entry to the first body paragraph and keep you from having to repeat yourself. The thesis sentence contains the main idea—the topic and the writer's angle on the topic—for the entire writing. The first sentence of each body paragraph—the topic sentence—should express the main idea—the subtopic—for only that paragraph. So, in the best-constructed writing, the thesis sentence is closely related to the topic sentences of each of the body paragraphs. And the thesis sentence is positioned right before the first topic sentence, so the one should lead right into the other. If you do not find such an easy transition in your writing, review the thesis sentence and the topic sentence of the first paragraph to make certain that the latter deals clearly with one facet of the thesis sentence and does not relate to another larger or unrelated issue.

Review how the transition occurs using the following example:

Forty-three students failed the state Test of Basic English Skills, while sixty-three students failed the state Test of Basic Math Skills. College entrance test scores hover consistently around the twentieth percentile, and only 10 percent of graduates attend four-year colleges. The student dropout rate for the last five years averages 15 percent. The dismal student performance levels of XYZ High School must be reversed, and only a state takeover of the school district can improve conditions.

The next paragraph should open with a topic sentence that contains one facet or subtopic of the topic revealed in the thesis sentence. This should work to continue the ideas expressed in the thesis sentence without repeating it, so subtlety, imagination, and knowledge of other areas related to the topic are required. Before composing a topic sentence, decide upon the subject of the first body paragraph, then write the

---

┏━━━━━━━━━━━━━━━━━━━━━━━━━━━━━━━━━━━━━━━━━━━━━━━┓

▭▬ QUICK TIP ▬▶

# The Thesis Sentence Is the Guidepost
## for the Writing

Place your main idea in the thesis sentence and begin each body paragraph
with a topic sentence that reflects some aspect of the thesis sentence.

┗━━━━━━━━━━━━━━━━━━━━━━━━━━━━━━━━━━━━━━━━━━━━━━━┛

main or topic sentence to reflect the paragraph subject. In the example
provided, the writer can either pursue the issue (1) that the dismal performance levels must be reversed, or (2) that a state takeover of the district will improve conditions. Both flow from the introduction, but
each tackles a different set of support ideas.

If the first portion of the thesis statement is the focus, then the writer
will examine the range of ways in which the performance levels on tests
could be improved, and the topic sentence of the first paragraph would
identify one of these ways to explore in the first body paragraph. For example: "The administration must allow teachers greater freedom to adapt their
instructional approaches according to the ability levels of each class."

If, on the other hand, the writer wishes to emphasize the value of a
state takeover to improve conditions, the support paragraphs will
develop points that exhibit the types of improvements to be expected.
Thus, the topic sentence of the first and later body paragraphs should
provide a detailed opinion on one type of improvement that the first
paragraph will examine. For example: "New rules and greater resources
that flow to our school once the state takes over running the district will
benefit both students and faculty."

If the writer chooses to change the thesis during the revision stage,
all of the topic sentences and the support details must also be assessed
and changed as appropriate, in order to create a consistent and coherent
writing.

**SELF-TEST**

Each set of sentences below consists of a thesis sentence and three
potential topic sentences for the same writing. Decide which sets

exhibit consistency and coherence between the thesis sentence and the three topic sentences and mark them with a "Y." Mark "N" those sets that do not contain consistency and coherence between the thesis sentence and the three topic sentences.

1.____ Strong leaders can mobilize the thinking of their followers and give even a dejected population the confidence that they can succeed.

   a. General George Washington convinced Revolutionary War soldiers that they could defeat the well-armed, precision-trained British army.

   b. United States President Franklin Delano Roosevelt raised the spirits of a nation suffering deep financial difficulties, which helped it to emerge from the Great Depression.

   c. Businessman Ross Perot ran as the Independent Party candidate for president of the United States in 1992.

2.____ Not everyone is willing to spend the long hours and take responsibility for all of the successes and failures that are part of owning a small business.

   a. The checks all go to the business owner, but so do the bills and complaints when something goes wrong.

   b. Social life must often be put aside to deal with business matters.

   c. Working for a large corporation offers security.

3.____ Teaching is a vital profession that should be considered more prestigious in this state.

   a. Most children spend more waking hours during the school year with teachers than with their parents.

   b. Teachers have provided the educational foundation for the thinking of even the most brilliant individuals.

   c. Training requirements in this state demand as much professionally of teachers as of any other more highly regarded profession.

4.____ Placing labels on rock music videotapes and compact discs to warn parents of their potentially dangerous lyrics and negative impact on adolescent children is an exercise in futility.

    a.  Adolescents have disposable income and purchase their own entertainment videotapes and CDs.

    b.  Parents watch and listen to many of the same videotapes and CDs without harm.

    c.  The material is easily available to adolescents in independent stores, where clerks do not "card" purchasers.

5.____ The concept of "family values" is hard to define for any given set of individuals, and politicians should stop trying to do so.

    a.  No one has the right or the ability to define for others what constitutes a family.

    b.  Living alone makes life much simpler.

    c.  Every closely associated group of people should create its own rhythms, ways of working together, and values.

## ANSWERS

Only one of the following sentence sets contains a thesis sentence with three correctly developed topic sentences, each serving as a subtopic of the thesis and expressing the views of the thesis.

1. _N_ Sentence C has the possibility of being rewritten to become a suitable topic sentence, but it is inconsistent with the other two topic sentences as currently phrased. Even though the statement refers to a politician who mobilized a group of people to vote for him and to join in the attempt to bring about reform, he is not an officially designated leader in the sense meant by the thesis and as indicated in the earlier two topic sentences.

2. _N_ The thesis sentence deals with the long hours and responsibilities of business ownership, views with which topic sen-

tences A and B are consistent. Topic sentence C fails to make reference to the issues raised in the thesis sentence, as it offers an alternative work situation. If the writer wants to keep in the writing a discussion of the security offered by working in a corporation, then the sentence must be revised to show how this subtopic of development is related to the thesis sentence. If working for a corporation is to be discussed as a preferable alternative, then the thesis and first two topic sentences must be rewritten and the writing drastically revised.

3. __Y__

4. __N__ The thesis sentence focuses on the use of warning labels to alert parents to potentially dangerous lyrics in order to provide them with a means of monitoring their adolescent children. Whether or not the parents watch the same music videotapes or listen to the same music is not at issue in the thesis sentence, so it should not be of concern in the topic sentences. The writer might make B into a suitable topic sentence by rewriting it to state that the material purchased by parents might be easily available in the homes of adolescents.

5. __N__ Sentence B may be true, but it does not provide a further point of development for the thesis sentence, which states that no one has the right to determine the values of any group. The thesis statement does not debate single versus communal or family life. Rather, the focus of the writing is to support the rights of families to determine values on their own.

## Writing a Strong Introduction

1. Decide how much information to reveal in the introduction before you write.
2. Select the opening approach (anecdotal, factual, question) that best allows you to develop the content.
3. Make the thesis sentence function as a transition from the introduction to the body paragraphs.

Using the techniques that you learned in this chapter, complete each of the following opening paragraphs by matching it with the correct thesis sentence. On the line preceding each paragraph, write the letter of the thesis sentence that matches the paragraph content.

1.\_\_\_\_ The computer systems now available provide the latest entertainment technology as well as the normally expected capabilities for processing documents, searching the Internet, and figuring out finances. Without leaving the computer station, we can watch movies on built-in DVD drives, enjoy the latest music or our favorite CDs, and follow our favorite sports teams in live-action broadcasts. The Internet helps us to save time and permits us to order anything from clothes to furniture, from gifts to take-out food.

a. Computers have taken control of our lives and destroyed what dignity we once had as human beings.

b. Life has become much more convenient and manageable as the result of the advances in computer capabilities.

c. People have become lazy because of their computers.

2.\_\_\_\_ Trees, a brook, and tiny animals played across the landscape of the green field in the distance. I had arrived in Dunbar the evening before, on a journey to recapture my roots and to see where my grandparents had lived sixty years ago before heading north to make their fortunes. The little southern town seemed to my eyes to have remained exactly as my grandparents had described it to me. The little general store was at the end of the one main street, as my grandfather had described. The clock tower of the city hall building still stood guard over the town square. My grandparents had been meticulous in using words to paint the beauty of the scene. I saw what they had seen, but as the white town residents began to eye my dark skin with suspicion, I also felt the ugliness that had forced my grandparents to leave the town.

a. No one should ever attempt to revisit the past, because it is always too painful.

b. The feeling reminded me that racism in small towns is more vicious than racism in large cities.

c. The irony of that feeling in the pleasant setting made me wonder if people ever truly change.

3.____ Where are the numerous investors who said they would stand by XYZ Corporation until we reached profitability? Who will subsidize the losses the company is suffering? Was the verbal handshake with our chief investor worth anything now? Who would have thought this could happen to a company billing $15 million annually?

a. In light of the bad economy and our major losses, the best course of action is for XYZ Corporation to close its doors and give up.

b. The lesson to be learned is that even the most well-supported business has to work to become recession-proof or expect to fail when the hard times hit.

c. We can blame no one but ourselves for this disaster.

## ANSWERS

1.__B__ The other two choices may be true, but key words in this paragraph express approval of the conveniences offered by computers, and the paragraph leads up to what must be a thesis sentence that also expresses approval.

2.__C__ The thesis sentences in A and B hold general truths, and they might be applicable to a writing that is more broadly based. In this instance, however, the limited scope presented by the writer demands a more specific thesis sentence.

3.__B__ The best course of action for the company may be to simply give up, as thesis sentence A states, and the company may be at fault for its financial problems, as thesis sentence C states. Despite these possibilities, such choices are dead-end thesis sentences, because they offer the writer no room for discussion and the reader no chance for growth. If the writer really does expect to examine the issue in additional paragraphs, then thesis sentence C is the only choice.

# 4 Building the Body Paragraphs

In this chapter you will learn to:

- write the well-constructed body paragraph

- select the most appropriate pattern of organization (example, narration, description, process analysis, comparison and contrast, analogy, cause and effect, or classification) to develop the writing

- effectively connect body paragraphs

Finding a topic, writing an introduction, and developing a thesis sentence are very important to writing clearly, but they are only the first steps. Your ideas must be well-supported, with details arranged in a logical pattern within each support paragraph, and must follow a specific pattern to effectively convince your readers that your writing is credible. Unlike the very specialized introduction and conclusion paragraphs, which must contain a sense of the entire writing, each body paragraph is a cluster of information related to just one aspect of the overall writing and should both support the main point of the writing and move the reader on to the additional paragraphs of support.

Body paragraphs must clearly express the position taken in the thesis sentence and must contain sufficient information to assure readers that the ideas discussed are valid and supportable. For this reason, the length of each paragraph is important. Too brief a paragraph will fail to inform readers, while too lengthy a paragraph will bury the main point in excess words.

Writing students frequently insist upon being assigned a minimum and maximum number of sentences for each paragraph. Those of us who teach writing resist providing such numbers, because the topic and your handling of it should determine how much you write. When pressed, however, we usually answer that each body paragraph should contain from five to seven or more well-developed sentences, but even that answer falls short because of the variation among topics. The best answer is that writers will know that they have struck the right balance if the discussion is coherent and each of the body paragraphs contains a clearly focused main idea, sufficient development to explain the main idea, and the appropriate organization to showcase the writer's ideas. Your goal is to keep readers interested and to make your point clearly.

# Writing Effective Body Paragraphs

Think of the body paragraphs as the building blocks that support the ideas and argument introduced in the opening of your writing. If they do not provide the substance and proof for your thesis, then readers will have no reason to believe in you or in what you have written. In short, without the building blocks, the writing is worthless.

The structure of each body paragraph is that of a brief essay. All elements should work together and support each other, as well as support the main idea of the essay. The topic sentence contains the main point of the paragraph (the introduction and thesis sentence condensed); the support sentences (similar to the body paragraphs in the essay) contain details to directly develop the topic sentence and, indirectly, the thesis sentence; and the clincher or concluding sentence works in the same way as the concluding paragraph of a larger writing. Examine the following body paragraph and imagine how you would edit the text to make the paragraph work as a unified whole.

Math is the school subject that has become most useful in my daily life, yet I hated all of my math classes in high school. Who could find a use for algebra or geometry then? French I and II were fun, because most of my friends were in the same classes with me both years. English was bearable. And I excelled in history. I also found physical education to be fun, because I have always been athletic. I never thought that the hours spent in class working out equations and figuring out sines and cosines or calculating the areas and perimeters of objects on paper would have any use. Does anyone ever really like high school? The regimentation may be good for some people, but I like to make my own rules and follow my own path. As a building contractor today, I have to use my geometry skills when planning how much lumber, flooring, and Sheetrock to order, or I lose money. I also use algebra equations to calculate how much I am paying for building materials and to decide which are the best deals. High school may not be for everyone, but it was good for me.

This body paragraph tries to compress too much information and deviates from the topic sentence at many points. The writer makes a promise in the topic sentence to discuss how useful math has become to his daily life, in contrast to his earlier hatred of high school math classes. As a result of the promise made in the topic sentence, the reader should expect that only these two aspects will be developed in the paragraph. Instead, the paragraph provides reviews of other high school courses and ends with a sentence that is too general to enhance the value of the present paragraph.

Here are some possible edits:

Math is the school subject that has become most useful in my daily life, yet I hated all of my math classes in high school. Who could find a use for algebra or geometry then? ~~French I and II were fun, because most of my friends were in the same classes with me both years. English was bearable. And I excelled in history. I also found physical education to be fun, because I have always been athletic.~~ I never thought that the hours spent in class working out equations and figuring out sines and cosines or calculating the areas and perimeters of objects on paper would have any use. ~~Does anyone every really like high school? The regimentation may be good for some people, but I like to make my own rules and follow my own path.~~ As a building contractor today, I have to use my geometry skills when planning how much lumber, flooring, and Sheetrock to order, or I lose money. I also use algebra equations to calculate how much I am paying for building materials and to decide which are the best deals. High school may not be for everyone, but it was good for me.

The paragraph becomes more unified as the sentences that are unrelated to the high school math classes are removed, and the coherence of the writing is increased. As the revised version of the paragraph exhibits, however, changes must still be made. Analyze the effect on understanding of the current concluding sentence and develop a sentence that more authoritatively ends the paragraph. *High school may not be for everyone, but it was good for me.* This concluding sentence is general enough to be used to end paragraphs containing discussions of a large number of topics, but it is not an effective concluding sentence for a paragraph on this specific topic. To be effective in ending this specific paragraph, the sentence should tie together the disparate elements appearing in the topic sentence, and refer to both the writer's earlier hatred of math and the unexpected recognition of how valuable math has become. For example: *What happened with math has taught me to be cautious and to not be so quick to condemn.*

Now revised, the sample paragraph provides a good example of the well-structured body paragraph. Use the following brief checklist in constructing your own successful body paragraphs:

1. Identify a main point to unify the paragraph.

2. Create a topic sentence to express the main point.

3. Select details relevant to the main point and place them in sentences that flow from one to the other and develop the topic sentence.

4. Remain focused on the topic—avoid the temptation to stray.

5. End the paragraph with a clinching sentence that both refers back to the details just presented and contains a transition to the topic sentence of the next paragraph.

The main point of a body paragraph should be a focused subtopic of the thesis sentence. Suppose that you were writing a paper with the following thesis sentence: *Self-appointed community censors should be stopped because their actions infringe upon the rights of others.*

What might be one strong supporting point to develop in the first body paragraph of the writing? You might choose to discuss first that the censors are just what they have been labeled—self-appointed—and that they represent only a limited viewpoint. The topic sentence of the first body paragraph must lead from the thesis sentence into the first point being discussed, in addition to being a summary of the main idea for the paragraph, and it tells readers what to expect as they continue. One possible topic sentence might be the following: *Groups or individuals who try to censor books or viewing materials in a community usually represent only a small segment of the population.*

Now what must you do? Either support the topic sentence with examples and details that provide a well-focused discussion of the main idea expressed in the topic sentence, or develop a new topic sentence that is supportable. Do not simply place information into the paragraph and hope that readers will not notice the padding, double-talking, and irrelevant information that sometimes passes for support. Strive instead to develop strong ideas that support the topic sentence—do not simply use ideas that depend upon it.

What are some ideas that you might develop into sentences to support the topic sentence above?

- Only one or a few people might object to a specific videotape, book, or compact disc, but the noise they make will lead others to believe that a larger number of people have protested.

- Censorship is unacceptable because differences in religious, cultural, and social experiences make nearly every source of entertainment a likely candidate for censorship to at least one person.

- Those who object to specific videotapes, books, or compact discs should use the power of the pocketbook or the library card to protect themselves and those close to them, rather than deprive others of the experience.

- Moral values differ among groups and families, and people should not be allowed to impose their moral values upon those who are outside of their group or family.

- The actions and entertainment sources of the group bringing a protest and raising a call for censorship are probably not above scrutiny, and they and their practices may also be likely candidates for censorship.

These choices would provide you with adequate relevant details to support the topic sentence that we devised earlier in the chapter. Each supports the main idea expressed in the topic sentence, and all are relevant to the overall intention of the writing as expressed in the thesis sentence.

What if you were to place all of the sentences containing potential support ideas into one paragraph? Would you have a well-written support paragraph? Probably not, because one sentence might duplicate the ideas of another, and seemingly consistent support details might contradict each other when placed in close proximity. Nonetheless, let us create a paragraph using the topic sentence developed earlier and the five potential support ideas.

> *Groups or individuals who try to censor books or viewing materials in a community usually represent only a small segment of the population.* Only one or a few people might object to a specific videotape, book, or compact disc, but the noise they make will lead others to believe that a larger number of people have protested. Censorship is unacceptable because differences in religious, cultural, and social experiences make nearly every source of entertainment a likely candidate for censorship to at least one person. Those who object to specific videotapes, books, or compact discs should use the power of the pocketbook or the library card to protect themselves and those close to them, rather than deprive others of the experience. Moral values differ among groups and families, and people should not be allowed to impose their moral values upon those who are outside of their group or family. The actions and entertainment sources of the group bringing the protest and raising the call for censorship are probably not above scrutiny, and their practices may also be likely candidates for censorship.

This paragraph, formed by simply combining the sentences, lacks unity and contains too much repetition of ideas, but it is a beginning. Read the sentences carefully. Decide where you must remove entire sentences. Which sentences can you rewrite or edit to maintain the idea but make its expression consistent with the topic sentence?

> *Groups or individuals who try to censor books or viewing materials in a community usually represent only a small segment of the population.* Only one or a few people might object to a specific videotape,

book, or compact disc, but the noise they make will lead others to believe that a larger number of people have protested. Censorship is unacceptable because differences in religious, cultural, and social experiences make nearly every source of entertainment a likely candidate for censorship to at least one person. <u>Those who object to specific videotapes, books, or compact discs should use the power of the pocketbook or the library card to protect themselves and those close to them, rather than deprive others of the experience.</u> Moral values differ among groups and families, and people should not be allowed to impose their moral values upon those who are outside of their group or family. The actions and entertainment sources of the group bringing the protest and raising the call for censorship are probably not above scrutiny, and their practices may also be likely candidates for censorship.

The underlined sentence makes a strong statement and provides specific ways in which self-appointed censors can make their views known without unfairly imposing their restrictions upon other members of a community. Because it contains both a summation of the topic and recommendations, this strongly worded sentence would work as an excellent first sentence for the concluding paragraph of the entire writing. However, placed in the body paragraph, it contributes nothing and only serves to disrupt the unity of the writing.

The paragraph requires editing beyond removing only the one sentence, even though the remaining sentences contain ideas that are relevant to the topic sentence. Review and edit the remaining sentences so that they are consistent in expressing the specific details to support the topic sentence.

*Groups or individuals who try to censor books or viewing materials in a community usually represent only a small segment of the population. Only one or a few people might object to a specific videotape, book, or compact disc, but the noise they make will lead others to believe that a larger number of people have protested. Censorship is unacceptable because differences in religious, cultural, and social experiences make nearly every source of entertainment a likely candidate for censorship to at least one person. [The preceding sentence makes an important point regarding the way in which religious, cultural, and social experiences influence what people choose to censor, but the fault lies in the way the support idea is phrased. The focus in the topic sentence and in the sentence containing the first specific support idea is on the people who seek to censor. In the preceding sentence, the writer places the focus on censorship. Rewrite the sentence as two sentences that separate the important ideas implied and make them consistent with the tone and form of expression of the first two sentences of the paragraph.]* Moral values differ among groups and families, and people should not be allowed to impose their moral values upon those who are outside of their group or family. *[This sentence also makes a valid point regarding the personal nature of censorship, but the way the thought is expressed obscures its value. Rewrite the sentence to make it consistent with the tone and form of expression of the first two sentences.]* The actions and entertainment sources of the group bringing the protest and raising the call for censorship are probably not above scrutiny, and their practices may also be likely candidates for censorship. *[The preceding sentence has the tone of a clincher or concluding sentence, but it requires editing to make it work and to lead into the next support paragraph.]*

The final version of the paragraph appears below and incorporates all of the suggested changes. The final sentence now serves the dual purpose of both concluding the first body paragraph and leading the reader into the next. Later in this chapter we will discuss how to make effective connections.

*Groups or individuals who try to censor books or viewing materials in a community usually represent only a small segment of the population and should not be allowed to make decisions for the majority.* Only one or a few people might object to a specific videotape, book, or compact disc, but the noise they make often leads others to believe that a larger number of people have protested. The censors tend to ignore the reality that differences in religious, cultural, and social experiences make nearly every source of entertainment worthy of censorship to at least one person. The same is true of those who hide behind the façade of "moral values" when seeking to censor. They should be prevented from imposing their values upon others, because the nature of what is "moral" differs among groups and even among families. No one

---

```
━━━▪ QUICK TIP ▪━━━▶
```

## Create Body Paragraphs That Are Unified and Complete

Treat each body paragraph as if it were a brief essay. Be certain to include a clear statement of the main idea (topic sentence), development of specific ideas (support sentences), and a conclusion (clincher sentence).

---

will deny a family or specific group the right to determine their own standards and values, but they should not be permitted to force the majority to follow their dictates, because even the standards and beliefs of the group bringing the protest may be likely candidates for censorship.

**SELF-TEST**

Read the following sample body paragraph and determine if it is unified and complete. Consider the following questions in your assessment and use them to guide you as you rewrite the paragraph:

*One of the most important qualities that a physician should have is the desire to help people.* Not everyone is likable, and many people are deliberately nasty, but everyone can use assistance at one time or another. A physician is expected to have medical expertise, but many people would also admit that they feel so much more cared for when their doctor treats them as individuals rather than as simply another fifteen-minute appointment. Although the general opinion is that all physicians are rich, drive big cars, and charge exorbitant fees, many are true healers who spend long hours comforting patients in hospitals and nursing homes. They give their elderly and troubled patients the time that they need, and ignore the fact that the HMO may only be paying a minimum fee and allowing them eight minutes per patient. Many people have no one in their lives on a regular basis other than their physician, in whom they grow to place a lot of trust. The physician who truly cares knows that caring is important.

• Does the topic sentence provide a clear statement of the main idea?

• Does each of the support sentences relate to the main idea?

• Do the support sentences contain specific details and ideas to develop the topic sentence?

• Does the final sentence serve as a conclusion to the paragraph?

• Do the sentences flow smoothly and logically?

_____

_____

_____

**ANSWERS**

The paragraph deals with a very important subject, and the writer shows compassion in writing about both physicians and patients. The main idea is clearly stated in a topic sentence that provides extensive possibilities. Most of the sentences that follow contain specific details and ideas to support the topic sentence, but, as phrased, some of the sentences are not relevant to this specific topic sentence. If rephrased, they can be made consistent with the main idea expressed in the topic sentence. The final sentence is weak and the double talk detracts from the important discussion. With revision, the sentences of the paragraph can be made to flow smoothly and logically.

Review the edited version of the paragraph that follows and compare it to your rewritten version. What did you omit? Why? What did you keep? Why?

*One of the most important qualities that a physician should have is the desire to help people.* ~~Not everyone is likable, and many people are deliberately nasty, but everyone can use assistance at one time or another.~~ *A physician is expected to have medical* expertise, but many people would also admit that they feel so much more cared for when their doctor treats them as individuals rather than as simply another fifteen-minute appointment. Although the general opinion is that all physicians are rich, drive big cars, and charge exorbitant fees, many are true healers who spend long hours comforting patients in hospitals and nursing homes. [*Rephrase this important support idea to serve as a detail that supports the topic sentence.*] They give their elderly and troubled patients the time that they need, and ignore the fact that the HMO may only be paying a minimum fee and allowing them eight minutes per patient. [*Rephrase this important support idea to serve as a detail that supports the topic sentence.*] Many people have no one in their lives on a regular basis other than their physician, in whom they grow to place a lot of trust. The physician who truly cares knows that caring is important. [*Strengthen this closing sentence and provide the important topic of this paragraph with a decisive conclusion.*]

Below is a more unified version of the sample paragraph that contains greater emphasis on the ideas that directly support the topic sentence.

*One of the most important qualities that a physician should have is the desire to help people.* A physician is expected to have medical expertise, but many people would also admit that they feel so much better cared for when their doctor treats them as individuals rather than as simply another fifteen-minute appointment. The true healers who spend long hours comforting patients in hospitals and nursing homes are physicians who value the intangible aspect of the profession. They give their elderly and troubled patients better care by allowing them the time that they need, and by ignoring the fact that the HMO may only be paying a minimum fee and allowing them eight minutes per patient. Many people have no one in their lives on a regular basis other than their physician, in whom they grow to place a lot of trust. Physicians who truly care for their patients do more than simply heal their bodies, they care for their feelings as well.

# Selecting the Most Effective Pattern of Development

Teachers of writing at all academic levels are often rigid in asking students to follow specific patterns of writing or methods of development throughout lengthy essays or a series of paragraphs. They assign students to write a "description essay," a "process analysis," a "classification writing," and so on, as if a writer will use only one pattern exclusively over the course of three hundred or more words. This is impossible, because every writing assignment contains a combination of patterns dictated by the needs of the individual body paragraphs. You may write a paper that compares and contrasts two or more ideas or items, but you cannot avoid including examples, discussing cause and effect, providing narration, and using other patterns for at least some of the paragraphs.

In the next few pages, as we review the most common patterns of development, keep in mind that these are not artificially created methods of development. Instead, they are based on the ways most people think when communicating ideas to another person. The pattern selected should be one that is suitable for a given topic, so consider your method of development carefully.

**Narration,** in which a writer tells a story, is the pattern of organization with which the majority of people feel most comfortable. From childhood on, we tell stories every time we answer the question "What happened?" The organizing principle of a narrative is time. Events occur in a given sequence, and the writer may choose to present the events in chronological order (in the order in which they occurred), in reverse chronological order (tell of a major event then work backward in time to relate how it all began), or with flashbacks (relate selective incidents that are important to the present event). In some writing situations, the intention of the writing as a whole is to narrate an event or a series of events, but to tell the story effectively the writer also uses many of the other organizational patterns. When narration is used for a support paragraph that is part of a larger writing, the entire paragraph is organized on that pattern. The following narrative is a brief story about a frightening sailing experience.

> Sailing had always been a fun-filled recreation for me, until the day that I learned the power of the water and the danger of my casual attitude. The October day was bright and sunny, a sailing

day like many before, even if the autumn breeze was cold. The car cassette player blasted songs by the Beach Boys as I drove to the lake with the little Sunfish skiff on my trailer. I was pleased to think that the lake would be deserted because of the colder temperatures, and I looked forward to the solitude. After going through the usual preparations, and debating whether or not to use the life jacket, I lowered the boat into the water and raised the sail. A brisk wind caught the sail and quickly moved the boat away from the shore, and a dark gray cloud appeared in the sky. The wind picked up, and the little Sunfish began to bounce around on the increasingly rough water as lake water saturated the sail. I was afraid for the first time in six years of sailing. The lake waters became choppy, and I worked desperately to lower the sail and to adjust the centerboard, to keep from swamping the boat, feeling grateful that I had decided to wear the life jacket. The little hull continued to bounce wildly on the rough water and to move rapidly toward the black waters of the middle of the lake. Terrified at that point, I grabbed the oar that was clamped under the seat and began rowing as quickly as I could. Shore was still within reach. Once on shore, I realized that I would never again be so casual about sailing. If I had waited longer to decide about coming in, the boat would probably have capsized in the middle of the lake, and no one would have found me in time because the lake was deserted, as I had hoped.

Another familiar pattern of organization that we also use frequently in conversation is **example.** Our explanations of people or events need illustrations, and carefully chosen examples provide them for our listeners and readers. The following paragraph contains one woman's explanation of her father's ambition and facility with language.

My father was a very ambitious man who worked hard to make a life for himself and his family. Soon after emigrating from Poland to the United States, he obtained a job as a laborer in a silk factory. Most of the other workers were Italian-born and even the supervisors spoke the Italian language. In order to keep up with the others, my father learned to speak fluently in Italian at the same time as he continued to improve his English-language skills. After a few years of hard work, he moved up to become a manager in the company. This took him off the factory floor and into his own office, complete with a secretary. His secretary had been born in France and spoke heavily accented English. To communicate better with her—and to impress her—my father learned to speak French, and eventually became fluent in this language as well.

**Description** is another common technique in conversation, and writers find that it is also a useful pattern of organization. We describe with the goal of re-creating for others a person, a place, or an item. A well-written description appeals to the senses, and uses concrete and specific details of sight, sound, smell, taste, and touch to duplicate as nearly as possible an experience for the listener or reader. This pattern of organization is similar to the narration method, because a narrative depends heavily upon specific details and appeals to the senses for success. The major difference between narration and description is that a specific time sequence defines the narration method, while the description method is focused on sense details and on creating a word picture of a person, a place, or an item. The following paragraph contains a description of the writer's memories of a favorite vacation site.

Union Lake is an artificially created body of water that has passed successfully for decades as being one of nature's creations. Summer mornings on the lakeshore contain a cacophony of natural music. Water lapping softly onto the seasonally replenished sand provides a gentle background melody to the sharp cries of birds, hidden safely as they emit their sounds from among the thick leaves of the lofty trees that ring the lake. The emerald green of the leaves contrasts sharply with the tan sand that rings the lake water, itself a clear, pale blue that deepens to black toward the lake center. The air on shore is always cool, even in the summer heat, because of the shade thrown by the trees. It smells faintly of pine because of the scrub pines that dot the shore sporadically. The lake waters are pristine, kept that way by the concerted efforts of residents in the region, who gratefully acknowledge their debt to the state parks commission and have invested their own money at adding private patrols to keep the shores clean and visitors aware of their concern.

The method of **process analysis** requires that a writer pay more attention to order in presenting specific details than is called for by the other patterns of organization. Unlike the of narration method, which relates an incident or series of incidents, process analysis consists of instructions to guide us, to provide step-by-step explanations in how to perform certain operations or how to assemble items, or to explain how something is made or done. Anyone who has experienced the frustration of attempting to follow poorly written and badly organized instructions in putting together something as seemingly simple as a toy understands the need to present the steps in chronological order. The paragraph below explains to readers the process that one writer follows in beginning to write each new work.

The process of writing has always been difficult, and I have struggled as I began every one of my fourteen published books. The best way to describe how I approach that first paragraph is that I dither. Unlike writers who procrastinate, who avoid the inevitable need to finally sit down and begin hitting computer keys in the hope of producing something intelligible each day, I dither. My dithering is very methodical, and I follow the same process for every book. The first step is to clear my writing area, by putting away books on their appropriate shelves, straightening up supplies, organizing my disks. After the immediate area in which I work leaves nothing more to be organized, I begin to pace, to walk between kitchen and computer for the numerous cups of coffee that remain half-finished, their contents turning cold with the milk forming a skin on the surface. This part of the process may take several hours, or it may last for several days, but I have to wait as long as the ideas take to move from churning about chaotically in my head to being tapped out on the computer keyboard. When I finally run out of ways in which to dither, I sit in front of the computer and begin, and I do not stop writing until the book ends itself.

Another familiar pattern of organization or method of explanation is the use of **cause and effect.** Whenever we explain why something happened, we are examining the possible causes for a result that we already know. In some cases, we consider a cause and examine the many effects that may result. The topic sentence of a paragraph that is developed using the cause-and-effect method should either identify a cause, then allow the rest of the paragraph to identify several effects, or identify an effect, and then allow the rest of the paragraph to identify several causes. The topic sentence of the paragraph below identifies the effects of hearing loss, and the support sentences of the paragraph discuss possible causes.

> People who have enjoyed perfect hearing through most of their lives are often devastated when they begin to experience hearing loss, which can have a variety of causes. Health problems, family history, and proximity to sustained loud noises all have a negative influence on hearing. Taking certain medications affects the nerves in the ear, which in turn deadens the eardrum to sound. Congenital hearing problems make hearing loss inevitable at a certain age, and medical alertness is required in order to lessen the influence of this factor. The most preventable cause of hearing loss is sustained loud noise, which accounts for much hearing loss in younger adults. Blasting car stereos, proximity to the operation of heavy equipment, and loud club and concert music take their toll. Although preventable, the hearing loss that results is not reversible. The time to prevent hearing loss is before it occurs, but most of us are having too good of a time to think about the result.

The use of **comparison and contrast** as a method of organization is easier than other methods for those writers who enjoy the structure inherent in this pattern. We instinctively look for similarities and differences in much of what we do in daily life. We compare prices, select one item over another, establish relationships, favor one subject over another, and do a lot more based upon the comparisons that we make. In writing, to **compare** is to consider both similarities and differences between two entities, but to **contrast** is to focus solely on differences. This method offers the writer two ways in which to organize the details used to compare and contrast. Using the **comparison-of-wholes** approach, the writer provides all of the details from first one entity, then all of the details from a second entity, and finally concludes the paragraph with a unifying statement. Using the **point-by-point** approach, the writer decides on specific aspects of the two subjects to be considered and proceeds methodically to assess the subjects on each point, one point at a time. Example A uses the comparison-of-wholes approach, and example B uses the point-by-point approach.

### Example A

The professions of teaching and acting are basically similar, although the surface glamour of the acting profession would seem to refute that belief. Teachers must always play a role in front of the classroom audience and take care to prevent any personal feelings from interfering with the main purpose of teaching, which is to impart knowledge. Standing in front of a class full of students, or strutting the floor which passes for a stage, a teacher must hold the attention of students or most efforts at conveying knowledge will fail. Teachers cannot choose the composition of their audience, but must play to the classes they are assigned. Actors are similarly passive in regard to the makeup of their audience, and they must also mask their personal feelings and simply play the role assigned. They must hold the attention of their audience. A key difference between the two professions is that, unlike teachers, actors do not have captive audiences, so the consequences of failure are more severe.

### Example B

The professional standards for beauticians in the 1950s were much higher than they are for hairstylists in independent salons today. Beauticians were held to a dress code, barred from chewing gum, and expected to report to work wearing clean white uniforms, polished white shoes, and neat hairstyles. Today's hairstylists dress as they wish, some favoring jeans, and others looking as if they were going to a dance club rather than work. Many smoke, to their clients' discomfort, and chew gum, and their hairdos are less likely to inspire clients than to make them fear what their own results might look like. Most beauticians in the 1950s were on salary, but they could make additional money through tips and through commissions if they sold various extra services, so they felt encouraged to take their time in giving clients facials and other treatments without feeling a need to rush on to the next client. In contrast, many hairstylists today work as independent practitioners, renting a station at a salon or working only on a commission basis. The result is that they feel compelled to work on as many clients as they can at one time, in order to make as much money as possible.

**Classification and division** patterns provide writers with opportunities to sort and make sense of diverse ideas or items (classification) and the chance to examine in detail one item by writing about its distinct parts (division). To accurately classify items into categories that make a clear point for the reader, you must create specific categories and remain consistent in your process of classification.

Gardening, the cultivation of plants in enclosed areas for ornamental purposes, is of three types. Trees and shrubs should be planted before more temporary plantings. This category contains both relatively permanent materials that will be green year-round such as evergreens, rhododendrons, and holly, as well as tropical and subtropical species that must be kept in a greenhouse or a home during the winter months. They usually provide the foundation for a garden and can be used to hide the unattractive features of a building. The second most popular type of gardening includes beds and borders, which often use perennials such as delphinium, impatiens, and various shrubs and annuals such as zinnias, phlox, and others that add color. Borders are long, narrow strips in a garden and contain a variety of plants, including perennials, annuals, and shrubs. Beds are made by planting groups of flowers or shrubs in one contained area to create a mass effect. A third type of gardening is the creation of special gardens, which may have various designs and various gardening styles. Among special garden designs are rock gardens, herb gardens, wildflower gardens, and water gardens. Different gardening styles include bonsai, the deliberate and artificial dwarfing of plants with special pruning techniques to give the appearance of aged, gnarled trees, and espalier, a technique in which trees or woody shrubs are planted close to a wall or trellis and trained to grow in a flattened manner.

Division requires the writer to take one entity—a person, place, item, or experience—and analyze its components in a consistent manner.

The "thrown-together" look that the rock ingénue affected was actually a fashion disaster, from her hair to her makeup and clothes. Her purple-and-pink hair, standing straight out from her scalp, made her look as if she had a fiber-optic lamp on her shoulders. The glowing fluorescent green-and-blue eyeshadow and cheek streaks served to make her face look like that of a child playing with paint, rather than the face of an aspiring rock diva. The clothes of her "thrown-together" look were the greatest failure, because they lacked the drama for which she had aimed, and instead looked simply old and worn. The total impression was sad rather than startling.

One of the most difficult patterns of organization to use in conveying information to the reader is the **analogy** method, which draws an extended comparison between two seemingly unlike entities. Identifying the ways in which one less familiar entity is similar to a more familiar entity enables the writer to convey a better understanding of the topic to the reading audience. The difficulty lies in making the right comparison that will reveal important information about the topic without completely confusing readers.

To understand the fear with which tuberculosis—the dreaded TB—was once regarded, you have only to take a look at the way in which society in the early 1980s treated people who were diagnosed with AIDS. The victims were blamed for having contracted the disease. Middle-class people living on farms or in small towns and the upper social classes viewed TB as a disease of the teeming city tenement, a disease bred and spread by the unwashed immigrants, not by "nice people." In both cases, public outcry called for the isolation of victims from the general population, who feared that they would be infected. Although they were shunned and isolated within health facilities, AIDS patients did not face being sent off to sanitariums, a fate that befell numerous sufferers of TB. Family members of TB patients felt isolation, as others feared contracting the disease by eating

---

════ QUICK TIP ════

# Select the Best Pattern of Organization for Your Topic

Choose the pattern of organization carefully, in order to make certain that the method provides the maximum means of communicating with readers. Not all of the patterns can be used with all topics, so choose wisely.

---

or drinking in their homes and sharing the same airspace, an ignominy which relatives of AIDS patients also experience. Eight decades separated the health concerns created by TB and AIDS, but so much in the social reaction remained the same. Antibiotics have taken the fear out of TB, and the same may someday be said of AIDS.

**SELF-TEST**

Writing demands flexibility in approaching topics and determining how to develop ideas in order to produce writing that readers will consider meaningful. Although all patterns of development are not suitable for every topic, several different methods can be used for the same topic, depending on what you seek to communicate. For each of the following topics develop three different topic sentences, each following a different pattern of organization. Write the name of the pattern of development on the line preceding each sentence, and place the topic sentences you create on the lines following each topic.

1. Military service

    A. _____

    _____

    _____

    _____

B. _____

_____

_____

_____

C. _____

_____

_____

_____

2.   Vegetarian diets

A. _____

_____

_____

_____

B. _____

_____

_____

_____

C. _____

_____

_____

_____

3. Automobile insurance

A. _____

_____

_____

_____

B. _____

_____

_____

_____

C. _____

_____

_____

_____

## ANSWERS (Answers will vary.)

1. Military service

A. example
Serving in the U.S. military can provide young men and women with numerous opportunities for developing career skills and creating a future.

B. description
Marine boot camp on Parris Island, South Carolina, was an experience that changed my life and provided me with a sense of accomplishment.

C. cause and effect

Many men have stated clearly that reinstatement of the draft will have damaging results on their educational and professional aspirations.

2. Vegetarian diets

A. narration

Nothing has been as traumatic in my life as the first time that I ordered a vegetarian dinner in a restaurant that was famous for its steak.

B. classification

People mistakenly consider all vegetarian diets to be the same, but they are wrong.

C. comparison and contrast

People who consistently follow a vegetarian diet are healthier in many areas than those who include substantial amounts of meat in their diets.

3. Automobile insurance

A. process analysis

Keeping automobile insurance rates down in this state requires planning ahead and adhering to a specific program.

B. analogy

Automobile insurance coverage in this state is as rare as a snowball in July.

C. example

Automobile insurance companies offer many benefits to people in this state.

# Connecting Body Sentences Effectively

Good writing flows smoothly and seamlessly from one sentence to the next and from one paragraph to another. In finely tuned writing, the correct juxtapositioning of ideas creates this flow, which results from the appropriate balancing of old information and new ideas, and support that enhances what has already been written.

Transition words and phrases are important to writing, but they have less impact on coherence than most inexperienced writers realize. Instead, well-constructed and coherent writing depends more upon a clearly stated main idea (thesis sentence); topic sentences that function as bridges between the thesis sentence and specific details in support paragraphs; and details within each paragraph that support the topic sentence. Writing is—or should be—a deliberate act of construction; it must be if the writer is to establish communication with readers. If you are writing only for yourself, then you do not need to have concerns about coherence, clarity, flow, and the like. However, if you write to communicate, as most people do, then the structure of your writing is vital.

An obvious sign that a writer is controlled by the subject rather than vice versa lies in the use of such forced transitions as "First, Second, Third, Later, Finally . . . ," and so on, to begin body paragraphs. Teachers of writing in high school courses and basic college English encourage inexperienced writers to use such terms to establish the order for readers, because they know that more sophisticated idea development is beyond the ability and the interest of most of their students. If you are working through this guide, you must want to produce better writing, so begin now to avoid such obvious attempts at ordering your ideas. Instead, let the way you present and organize your ideas do the job.

The repetition of key words and the use of parallel sentence structure are important techniques to enhance coherence in your writing. The topic of the writing determines the specific key words to repeat judiciously throughout. If you are writing in favor of or against capital punishment, repetition of the term "justice for all" might be important. Read the following paragraph to see how one writer has repeated the word "mystery" and its variations to enhance the unity of the paragraph.

Murder *mysteries* fascinate me in a way that serious and scholarly literature never has. Investigation of dramatic structures of famous plays and analyses of the *mysteries* hidden in beloved novels may hold my attention for a time, but I would gladly trade a thousand obscure footnotes for one "clue" that will send my mind off in hot pursuit of someone's fictional criminal. *Mysteries* are my brain candy, despite the disdain with which my colleagues view such reading, some declaring that it is a *mystery* to them how I can enjoy such rubbish and even more of a *mystery* that I reveal this vice without shame. What they do not understand—

and I choose not to tell them—is that my love of *mystery* is the perfect companion to my love of research. I am the investigator in both activities, vicariously hunting the felon in someone's *mystery* novel, and the hunter of scholarly truths and fact on my own. The *mystery* is that no one but me has realized this yet.

The use of parallel sentence structure to create coherence requires a little more skill, because content sense must accompany parallel grammatical structure. In the following paragraph, the writer uses sentences of the same length and structure to signal unity between key ideas.

*The heart pounds. The blood rushes into the ears. The throat constricts. The muscles tense.* Health alert? Hardly. Instead, these are the symptoms of "write fright," a condition that afflicts ordinarily healthy individuals who are required to produce an essay, a letter, or a report within a given period of time. Such people speak eloquently on the telephone, and *they dazzle in e-mail.* Their downfall occurs when they are asked to create a formal writing. [*The italicized brief sentences in lines 1 and 2 contain important ideas set into a parallel grammatical structure, which provides coherence to the opening. The author also enhances the coherence of the next-to-last sentence by linking two sentences that are parallel in structure.*]

Although the body paragraphs should be connected by strongly written topic sentences that lead the reader from one paragraph to another, transition words that connect sentences can be used to enhance coherence and consistency within each paragraph. Transition words must be chosen carefully so that your writing will signal the correct connection between ideas, and will maintain the correct tone. To refer to preceding nouns, use pronouns alone or in conjunction with a more general category to which the original noun belongs to provide continuity without repeating the noun.

*Orangutans* are very similar to humans in their social interactions. *These primates* form family groups and care for their young much like we do.

Numerous words and phrases are also useful in providing transitions between sentences within your paragraphs. The table below contains a list of transition words and phrases arranged according to their functions. Learn the subtle differences between any transition words you might have confused in the past, and use all transition words and phrases judiciously. Keep in mind that transition words and phrases are tools to enhance the flow of your words—they are not meant to take the place of strong organization and a complete development of ideas.

| Transition Words and Phrases | Function |
| --- | --- |
| again, also, and, besides, further, furthermore, in addition, moreover, next, too | to indicate the addition of information |
| accordingly, as a result, consequently, for this reason, hence, if, since, so, then, therefore, thus | to exhibit causes and effects |
| also, by comparison, in the same manner, likewise, similarly | to indicate similarities |
| although this may be true, certainly, even though, granted, it is true, naturally, of course, to be sure, to tell the truth, with the exception of | to acknowledge the validity of another person's point |
| after all, but, however, in contrast, in spite of, nevertheless, on the contrary, on the other hand, still, unlike, yet | to prepare for a contrast |
| for example, for instance, in fact, to illustrate, specifically | to indicate examples |
| above, around, below, beyond, close, elsewhere, farther on, here, nearby, opposite, there, to the left (right) | to indicate place or direction (especially useful in spatially organized writing) |
| after, afterward, as, at the same time, before, currently, during, earlier, finally, formerly, immediately, in the meantime, lately, later, meanwhile, next, shortly, simultaneously, soon, subsequently, this time, until now, when, while | to provide indication of time or sequence |

---

```
▅▅▅▭ QUICK TIP ▬▬▬►
```
# Connect Your Thoughts

Make your writing coherent and more powerful by using the repetition of key words, pronoun references to important nouns, and transition words between sentences within the body paragraphs.

---

**SELF-TEST**

Review the following paragraph and identify the writer's use of transition words and expressions. Explain how each connecting device functions in the paragraph.

The process of writing has always been difficult, and I have struggled as I began every one of my fourteen published books. The best way to describe how I approach that first paragraph is that I dither. Unlike writers who procrastinate, who avoid the inevitable need to finally sit down and begin hitting computer keys in the hope of producing something intelligible each day, I dither. My dithering is very methodical, and I follow the same process for every book. The first step is to clear my writing area, by putting away books on their appropriate shelves, straightening up supplies, organizing my disks. After the immediate area in which I work leaves nothing more to be organized, I begin to pace, to walk between kitchen and computer for the numerous cups of coffee that remain half-finished, their contents turning cold with the milk forming a skin on the surface. This part of the process may take several hours, or it may last for several days, but I have to wait as long as the ideas take to move from churning about chaotically in my head to being tapped out on the computer keyboard. When I finally run out of ways in which to dither, I sit in front of the computer and begin, and I do not stop writing until the book ends itself.

**ANSWER**

The process of writing has always been difficult, and I have struggled as I began every one of my fourteen published books.

The best way to describe how I approach that first paragraph is that I *dither. Unlike* writers who procrastinate, who avoid the inevitable need to finally sit down and begin hitting computer keys in the hope of producing something intelligible each day, I *dither.* My *dithering* is very methodical, and I follow the same process for every book. The first step is to clear my writing area, by putting away books on their appropriate shelves, straightening up supplies, organizing my disks. *After* the immediate area in which I work leaves nothing more to be organized, I begin to pace, to walk between kitchen and computer for the numerous cups of coffee that remain half-finished, their contents turning cold with the milk forming a skin on the surface. *This* part of the process may take several hours, or it may last for several days, but I have to wait as long as the ideas take to move from churning about chaotically in my head to being tapped out on the computer keyboard. *When* I finally run out of ways in which to *dither,* I sit in front of the computer and begin, and I do not stop writing until the book ends itself.

The writer repeats the key word "dither," and its variation "dithering," to remind the reader of the topic. The time transition words "after" and "when" provide a sequence for the activity (or lack of it), and use of the term "unlike" allows the writer to contrast the process described, "dithering," with similar actions for which it may be mistaken. The pronoun "this" in conjunction with "part of the process" reminds the reader that the process of "dithering" is under discussion.

---

## Write Powerful Body Paragraphs

1. Create body paragraphs that are structured like essays
2. Select the most effective pattern of development for each body paragraph
3. Connect sentences within the body paragraphs by using repetition, pronouns, and transition words

Read each of the following support paragraphs carefully. Review the organization of the paragraph and determine if it meets our writing criteria for effective body paragraphs:

1.  Is the message of the body paragraph unified and complete?

2.  Is the pattern of organization appropriate for the topic?

3.  Are the sentences connected in a coherent manner?

Write a corrected version in which you place sentences in the correct order, provide transitions where they are needed, and eliminate unnecessary sentences.

### Example A

Researchers report that smaller class size provides a better learning environment for students in public schools. Personal attention is an important factor in encouraging student learning. When the teacher-to-student ratio is lower, students receive more personal attention. Behavior problems decrease when the teacher has fewer students to supervise. Students are less likely to act up when their actions are readily and easily seen. Individual assistance in classroom subjects is possible in small classes. The success rates of small classes should encourage schools nationwide to reevaluate their education programs.

_____

_____

_____

### Example B

Gaining the support of the city for the new baseball field was not difficult, but it did take planning and determination. Many people were against building a new field. No open land was available. Taxes are already too high in town. The town wanted to sell the only parcel of land that it had in order to increase tax ratables. A small committee of dedicated parents lobbied the town council. Many people signed a petition. Children sold candy and washed cars to raise money. The city considered the proposal and voted to turn the city-owned land into the much-needed baseball field. Parents and children appeared at several town council meetings to voice their request. People wrote letters to state and county officials, as well as to city officials, to ask for money to build the field.

_____

_____

_____

## ANSWERS

### Example A

The paragraph appears to have all the information needed to develop the topic sentence that begins it. The writer's use of *example* as the pattern of organization provides an effective method of development for this topic. Coherence is increased by placing several of the sentences in a different order and adding transition words to the beginnings of sentences to create consistency.

Researchers report that smaller class size provides a better learning environment for students in public schools. When the teacher-to-student ratio is lower, students receive more personal attention, which is an important factor in encouraging student learning. Behavior problems *also* decrease when the teacher has fewer students to supervise, *because* students are less likely to act up when their actions are readily and easily seen. Individual assistance in classroom subjects and attention to students' needs are possible in small classes. Because of these findings and the success rates of small classes, schools nationwide should reevaluate their education programs.

## Example B

The paragraph appears to contain the necessary information required to support the topic sentence, but the organization of the material requires revision. The writer relates the process by which parents and children convinced a town to build a baseball field, so the use of *process analysis* as the pattern of organization is appropriate. Several of the sentences required editing to provide needed transitions between thoughts, but no changes have been made to the parallel sentence structure in which key ideas are voiced in succinct statements.

> Gaining the support of the city for the new baseball field was not difficult, but it did take planning and determination. Many people were against building a new field. Many asserted that no privately owned open land was available. Others complained that taxes are already too high, so the town should sell the only parcel of land it had in order to increase tax ratables. Undeterred, people in favor of a baseball field mobilized their forces. A small committee of dedicated parents lobbied the town council. Many people signed a petition. Children sold candy and washed cars to raise money. Parents and children appeared at several town council meetings to voice their request. People wrote letters to state and county officials, as well as to city officials, to ask for money to build the field. After being bombarded with the demands, the city considered the proposal and voted to turn the city-owned land into the much-needed baseball field.

# 5 Concluding the Writing

## Objectives

In this chapter, you will learn to:

- avoid an ineffective conclusion

- structure an effective conclusion

- summarize without being redundant

- raise related issues and provide recommendations for further consideration

A good conclusion does more than simply end a piece of writing—it is also the last part of the writing that your readers will see. Even though it may be brief, the ending to your writing should leave a strong, positive impression with your readers. So if you have always viewed the conclusion as just a summary of what has been said earlier, and as only a few sentences to be dashed off and tacked onto the end of your prose, you might want to revise your thinking.

Many writers consider their job done if they have fully introduced readers to their topic, provided a clear intention for the discussion to follow, and developed ideas and organized them in a manner to convey the necessary information. Because the conclusion is the last paragraph in the writing, too many writers tend to treat it as an afterthought, a necessary evil that need not take much time or effort. That approach can sabotage a carefully planned and executed writing and destroy a writer's credibility. Rather than take that risk, work as hard in producing a solidly constructed, well-developed concluding paragraph as you would in creating the entire writing. The results are well worth it.

# Avoiding the Ineffective Conclusion

The conclusion of any writing may be harder to write than the introduction or the body paragraphs. With an introduction, you have a clean slate and all the possibilities of the topic ahead of you. The body paragraphs are subdivisions of that topic, and the approach you take in organizing your writing is often helpful in determining the information that must next be included in a body paragraph. The conclusion, however, must somehow reflect and interpret the entire writing.

Never attempt to write a conclusion without taking the time to review the introduction. The introduction paragraph promises readers that the writing to follow will explain a given topic from the specific angle stated in the thesis sentence. As the body paragraphs are written, the writer either does or does not fulfill those promises, depending upon how closely he or she follows the thesis sentence. By the time the writer reaches the final paragraphs, the original plan for the writing may have been forgotten or put aside; the moment of truth arrives when the conclusion must be written.

Even though it may be relatively brief compared to the piece as a whole, or even to the introduction, the conclusion must pack a punch. Leave your readers convinced that their time has not been wasted, but well spent. The conclusion should remind readers of the key issues they have reviewed and the important points you have made.

Do not depend on the conclusion to make readers think as you do about the topic if your writing to that point has not already been convincing. Instead, work to produce a conclusion to reinforce the arguments and points presented in the writing, one that assures readers that you believe in the importance and the soundness of what you have written and that you endorse your own ideas.

Above all, avoid the mistakes made by many insecure writers who are frightened of being exposed as either inexperienced or insincere. They either apologize to readers in the conclusion or write some version of the following: "The final views on this issue must be left to the reader."

As a writer, how can you expect the rest of your writing to be perceived as sound and valid if your conclusion is casual or noncommittal? Why waste time and effort to analyze an issue and to carefully structure a written discussion that may be several paragraphs or more in length, only to conclude that your views are of little importance to readers, who should make up their minds anyway? Put more bluntly, why waste your readers' time? Readers will feel betrayed if a writer apologizes for not having presented a strong enough analysis, for having too limited a knowledge of the subject, or for any other failings that readers may or may not have identified. Think about what such apologies tell readers. Think about what such apologies reveal about the writer.

The conclusions below are taken from the essays of first-year college composition students. The examples are chosen to illustrate the problems that many inexperienced writers face in trying to end their writings on a positive note, and they exhibit the damage that weak or noncommittal conclusions can do.

## Example 1

In conclusion, that's all that I have to say about the topic, and I'm not sure that there is really anything more to write about. Capital punishment means taking another life, and I am against taking a life for any reason. But we all have to make up our own minds about this issue.

Identify the weaknesses of the preceding conclusion, and explain what the writer can do to strengthen it.

_____

_____

_____

Opening the paragraph with the words "In conclusion" is not sufficient to make the accumulation of words that follow an effective conclusion. The writer signals to the reader that the end is reached *not* because the issue has been comprehensively or even adequately explored; rather, she has run out of ideas. In an effort to establish a connection with readers, and to excuse what she relates as the lack of any further ideas to examine, she includes the statement "I'm not sure that there is really anything more to write about." Readers may take a different view, depending upon how complete the preceding writing has been. Nonetheless, the writer should not state so bluntly in the conclusion that the end has come because the well of ideas has run dry. Instead, the conclusion should be crafted to appear that the writer has completed the work that was promised in the introduction. The second sentence suggests that whatever else comes before the final paragraph in this effort is simply a concession to readers. The writer implies that the assignment compelled her to appear as if she wanted to play fair and to explore the issue, but that her views can be summed up in the following statement: "Capital punishment means taking a life, and I am against taking a life for any reason." Had this statement appeared in the introduction paragraph as the thesis sentence, the writing would have been more powerful and the conclusion more accurate. Instead, the essay compared different views regarding the issue of capital punishment, offering points both in favor of and against the issue. The conclusion fails to indicate that so comprehensive an examination occurred and that contrasting points appeared. As a result, any well-written and well-supported writing is undermined by a weak ending.

## Example 2

What's left to write about? So many aspects of the controversy over racial profiling have been discussed in the newspapers and on television that writing anything more would be redundant. Even the ideas discussed in this paper feel as if they are only rehashed arguments, so I have eliminated some of the details to avoid being boring. The point is that human nature is hard to change, and nothing that any student or I write about racial profiling will make a difference.

Identify the weaknesses of the preceding conclusion, and explain what the writer can do to strengthen it.

_____

_____

_____

The writer of this effort appears determined to convince readers that what he has written is not worth reading. If, after writing about an issue, you are tempted to produce a conclusion that even vaguely resembles this one, tear up your work and begin over with a new topic and a new perspective. The writer who believes that everything has already been said about the topic and that nothing of importance is left to consider should not waste his own time if "anything more would be redundant" and only "rehashed arguments" remain. Select another topic, if the choice is available. Even if the topic is assigned and another topic is not an option, the writer still owes himself and his readers an honest effort. Make the introduction work for you in identifying where you stand in regard to the issue. Do you believe that the topic has been needlessly magnified or distorted by media attention? If you do, then state this in the thesis sentence and let that approach guide the writing. If the assignment requires you to identify and to analyze the arguments that have been posed regarding racial profiling, do so. You can create your own angle on the issue and select specific support details from among the abundance of information that exists. Read the last sentence of this conclusion. The writer appears to express a strong and honest observation in the final sentence that might have functioned admirably as a thesis sentence for the entire writing, had he taken the time to write a first and even second draft of the paper and then edited and revised the material. As it stands, the conclusion paragraph seems to be the culmination of the writer's thinking, and the true thesis of the writing appears to be expressed in that final sentence. Because many student papers are written at the last minute before submission, the writer may have submitted only a first draft. Had he revised the material, the conclusion might have revealed a more significant effort.

## Example 3

Colleges must pay more attention to the education that they are providing their student athletes, and not just to their involvement in various sports. Of course, not all student athletes suffer academically, and many do very well in life after college. Each case is individual, and no one can safely generalize about the situation of athletics and academics at the college level.

Identify the weaknesses of the preceding conclusion, and explain what the writer can do to strengthen it.

In two sentences, the writer destroys what the strong opening sentence of the conclusion suggests may have been a well-written and well-supported essay. The strongly worded opening sentence is direct in expressing an opinion, and it probably reflects the thesis sentence and the development of the topic throughout the writing. The writer expresses a mandate to the colleges, and suggests that colleges exhibit too great a concern for the performance of student athletes on the field rather than in the classroom. In the second sentence, however, she backtracks and undermines the strong preceding sentence, leaving the reader unsure of her convictions. Does she even have an opinion about the way in which colleges treat their student athletes? What is that opinion? Is the final sentence a serious expression of frustration with the issue—or is the writer simply asking readers not to blame her if they do not view her opinions as valid? Even if the writer does not seek to avoid responsibility for the opinions she may have expressed, the addition of the statement "Each case is individual, and no one can safely generalize about the situation of athletics and academics at the college level" seems intended to remove from her all responsibility and blame for the statements she has made.

These examples of failed conclusions are only three among many types of errors made by writers who either underestimate the importance of the conclusion to the overall writing or who find that composing the conclusion is the hardest part of writing. Before we examine a range of ways in which to end your writing effectively, review the following cautions of what not to do. Avoid these three errors:

1.  Do not apologize to your reader for either the quality of your writing or for the lack of strength and development of support ideas. If the writing is so badly executed and the material so poorly developed that it warrants an apology to readers, then take the time to revise and to rewrite the material and improve it.

2.  Avoid the temptation to open new topics or to introduce new ideas in the conclusion. The accumulation of ideas in a lengthy

---

```
━━━━┐ QUICK TIP ━━━━
```
# Avoid Conclusion Pitfalls

1. Don't make excuses for weak content.
2. Don't plead ignorance or topic exhaustion.
3. Don't introduce new ideas at the end.

---

examination of a topic will frequently stimulate other possibilities for discussion. As you read through your work and make revisions, decide if the new ideas would enhance the writing and add to readers' understanding. If they would, then revise the entire writing to integrate the new information into the text and to develop it as a part of the overall writing. Do not include it solely in the conclusion paragraph. Such additions placed into the conclusion weaken the larger writing, making the work appear to be disjointed.

3. End your writing on a positive note, with a conclusion that maintains the energy of the writing to the end. Limp conclusions that seek to fade away unnoticed will receive substantial attention when they disappoint readers. A weak or indeterminate conclusion comes as a letdown and calls into question the convictions and the abilities of the writer. How can someone who really believes in what she or he has written in the preceding four hundred or more words simply walk away from the topic without taking one final opportunity to make certain that readers clearly understand their views on the issue? A weak ending creates doubt in the minds of readers and calls into question your credibility.

**SELF-TEST**

Read each of the following conclusion paragraphs and identify the errors made by the writer. Using the information provided, rewrite the paragraphs to create strong concluding statements.

### Example A

In summary, the ideas presented about raising the speed limits on highways to 70 m.p.h. presented in this writing are valid and very important to consider. You may not agree, but I have proved through the presentation of statistics from states that have raised their speed limits that traffic fatalities do not increase and that benefits actually result. The concept is one that all states should consider. States should also think of giving drivers specific incentives for maintaining good driving records.

---
---
---

### Example B

I really believe that television advertising assumes that viewers are not really very intelligent. Although I watched over forty hours of television at different times, I couldn't find any differences in advertising approaches between times of the day or different television stations. All I saw were products being sold in ways that really didn't respect the intelligence of viewers. That is really very sad.

---
---
---

## ANSWERS

### Example A

Avoid using such obvious attempts at transition as "in summary," "in conclusion," "finally," "as I have shown," and similar phrases. Instead, create a strong first sentence that actually summarizes the writing and relate that summary to concepts that have been presented in the paper. End the paragraph with a sentence that rings with finality and leaves no doubt in the reader's mind that this is, indeed, the end.

### Rewritten Example A

Raising the speed limit to 70 m.p.h. on highways nationwide has been shown to be a good idea. States that have already done so report no increases in fatalities and, indeed, they have even seen positive benefits such as a decrease of road rage incidents in recent months. Given the results, the concept is one that all states should consider.

## Example B

The writer uses the phrase "I really believe" in the attempt to convey sincerity, but the reader is led to wonder why a writer would write anything that is not to be believed. Should other ideas presented in the writing be questioned? The writer also apologizes for a lack of material to discuss, another concern for the reader, who may begin to feel that the writer is merely wasting her time if no differences among advertisements are found within forty hours of television viewing. The generalized state of the information is acceptable for the conclusion, and a fairly respectable ending can be contrived, but the original ending does call into question every thought and support point that the writer has used in the body paragraphs.

### Rewritten Example B

The advertising industry assumes that television viewers are either too unintelligent to see that they are being scammed or too lazy to change the channel when an advertisement that is insulting to their intelligence appears. This approach is consistent across the board and does not differ by time slot nor according to television market. Such disrespect for consumers in the United States saddens me, and it should sadden everyone. Perhaps the time has come for consumers to strike back with their pocketbooks and put the financial crunch on advertisers who disrespect them.

# Structuring the Effective Conclusion

Introductions and concluding paragraphs have their own set of rules for thought development. In contrast, body paragraphs are structured in the same manner as an essay—**introduction** (topic sentence containing the main idea of the specific paragraph), **support** (sentences that contain the specific details to support the topic sentence of the paragraph), and **conclusion** (final sentence of a body paragraph that serves as a bridge to complete the paragraph and lead the reader to the next paragraph).

The introduction and conclusion have different structures because of their different functions. As you will recall from chapter 3, the introduction establishes the context for the writing and moves from initial statements to set the stage for the **thesis sentence,** which ends the introduction and expresses the main idea of the overall writing (the topic and the writer's angle on the topic). The conclusion has a different function. By the time the writer reaches the end, all of the information has been given. The conclusion must sum up, make sense of the topic, suggest further uses for it, and identify ways in which readers might examine areas of the topic that remain untouched in the current writing. The task is weighty, yet most conclusions are relatively brief, containing only a few sentences, rarely more than five.

Each sentence in the conclusion has its role, and each idea must be carefully expressed to complete the message for readers, not to leave them feeling as if the writer has left something out. Make the conclusion as powerful as the introduction—and make it appear to be as simple and straightforward. To do this, you really must understand what you have written in the introduction and the body. You cannot simply sit down and write whatever comes to mind, then leave this as your final copy of the writing. The conclusion will not just come to you without considerable work and a thorough understanding of the material preceding it. Solid, relevant conclusions are difficult to compose.

Read your introduction paragraph many times to make the thesis come alive to you. Read through the body paragraphs to remind yourself of the ways the thesis sentence is supported by the topic sentence of each paragraph, and how each topic sentence is, in turn, supported by the sentences of a given body paragraph. Above all, familiarize yourself with the promises you made to the reader in the introduction and construct a conclusion to show that those promises have been kept.

The following introduction paragraph, thesis sentence, and topic sentences were written to examine the topic of "Consumerism." The writer chose to focus on the specific issue of "planned obsolescence." Read the introduction paragraph, thesis sentence (italicized), and topic sentences to become familiar with the issue and the approach that the writer has taken in examining the issue. Determine the angle that the writer must take in concluding the work, then decide whether Conclusion A, B, or C below the work best concludes this paragraph. Explain why the other two paragraphs are inadequate or inappropriate conclusions.

Buy a new piece of electronic equipment today, and you can expect it to last no longer than the warranty. Service contracts are time-limited, and many companies will only permit a consumer to purchase or renew contracts for up to five years after the purchase of certain equipment. *We are becoming a disposable society, and planned obsolescence appears to be built into everything we purchase.*

## Topic Sentence 1

Most families have telephones, but few have owned the same telephone for more than a few years, because the equipment manufactured over the last three decades is far less durable than the old black telephones made by Bell that once occupied most homes.

## Topic Sentence 2

Working radios and television sets from the first half of the twentieth century have become prized classic collectibles, but the same will not be said of the compact disc players and video-cassette recorders of today, because they usually do not work beyond five years.

## Topic Sentence 3

Classic car parades of the future will probably contain the same cars that are today considered classics, because the functioning lives of today's new models are limited.

Decide which of the following best concludes the writing:

## Conclusion A

Many more examples of our increasingly throwaway society do exist, but they do not come to mind at present. Nonetheless, we can expect that manufacturers will continue to produce goods that will last only a predetermined amount of time before they break and must be replaced. Our economy has come to depend upon such planned obsolescence to keep the wheels of industry turning.

## Conclusion B

Manufacturers of all types have built their individual economies on the principle of planned obsolescence. Moreover, the continued success of industry in the United States seems to be linked to society's continued willingness to discard. A return to the durable consumer goods of a generation or two ago is no longer practical, because production levels and jobs depend upon the constant consumer cycle to purchase items, discard items, and purchase anew. As a result, we have become victims of our own efficiency.

## Conclusion C

There is nothing more to be said about this topic, except to mourn for the changes that will result. The days of spending lazy afternoons strolling through antiques stores in country towns will come to an end, because too few items will last long enough to be labeled "classic." Aldous Huxley foresaw this day in his 1932 novel *Brave New World,* in which the inhabitants of Utopia were compelled to consume a certain amount of goods per year "in the interests of industry" and the propaganda stated that "Ending is better than mending."

Conclusion A and conclusion C deal with the issue presented in the introduction paragraph, but each contains specific errors that detrac from its value as a closing paragraph for the writing.

## Conclusion A

Many more examples of our increasingly throwaway society do exist, but they do not come to mind at present. [*This conclusion paragraph opens on a note of weakness and lessens reader confidence in the handling of the topic.*] Nonetheless, we can expect that manufacturers will continue to produce goods that will last only a predetermined amount of time before they break and must be replaced. [*The placement of this sentence raises questions about the seriousness of the writer, who has just admitted a failure to adequately brainstorm additional examples, then casually continues by using "nonetheless" to begin the next sentence. The thought expressed in this sentence is closely tied to the reason given in the following sentence, so a connector should be used between the two to strengthen the point.*] Our economy has come to depend upon such planned obsolescence to keep the wheels of industry turning. [*The paragraph should end with a sentence that expresses a more final opinion.*]

## Conclusion C

There is nothing more to be said about this topic, except to mourn for the changes that will result. [*The writer should reiterate the topic in some form, rather than generalizing and compelling the reader to reconnect with the introduction paragraph.*] The days of spending lazy afternoons strolling through antiques stores in country towns will come to an end, because too few items will last long enough to be labeled "classic." [*The writer makes a major leap without transition from mourning the demise of antiques stores to*

---

◢◀▭▭▭ QUICK TIP ▬▬▶

# Customize Your Conclusion

Write a conclusion paragraph that is made for your specific writing alone. Reread the introduction paragraph to recall what you promised readers and to make certain that the conclusion ends by doing what you started out to do.

*complimenting author Aldous Huxley for being a visionary. One point or the other must either be eliminated or vastly revised.*] Aldous Huxley foresaw this day in his 1932 novel *Brave New World,* in which the inhabitants of Utopia were compelled to consume a certain amount of goods per year "in the interests of industry" and the propaganda stated that "Ending is better than mending." [*The literary reference is interesting but, as phrased, it destroys the aim of unity for the concluding paragraph. A final sentence that definitively ends the paragraph is required.*]

**SELF-TEST**

Carefully examine the thesis sentences (in italics) in these examples and the corresponding topic sentences. Decide what information must be included to conclude the writing and how that information should be presented. Write your own concluding paragraph for each example and take care to avoid the pitfalls of ineffective conclusions.

## Example A

Home economics departments in high schools and colleges have long suffered from an image problem. In the 1950s and early 1960s, when every woman was expected to emulate television moms such as June Cleaver (*Leave It to Beaver*) and Donna Stone (*The Donna Reed Show*), classes were filled with girls making the mandatory brownies, learning housekeeping tips, and developing sewing skills, yet it was still a subject meant only for girls. Even when the occasional male student would take "Home Ec," once the liberated 1960s and 1970s emerged, it continued to suffer from being viewed as a low-priority class. *The old view is now long gone, and home economics has taken on a new image and emerged with a new mission that justifies its reclassification in formal education circles as a "practical art."*

## Topic Sentence 1

Many home economics departments have renamed themselves as "Home Management Skills" or "Domestic Management" departments.

### Topic Sentence 2

Cooking, baking, and sewing have given way to classes that focus on developing and implementing personal budgets, life management skills, home decorating, and food preparation safety.

### Topic Sentence 3

Many high school programs are working with local community college programs to integrate programs and to provide dedicated students with a means of seamless entry into the professional skills programs at the colleges.

_____

_____

_____

## Example B

The soft jazz tune plays soothingly in the background. Elegantly attired couples sit in the dim room and gaze lovingly across small round tables complete with rosebud vases. A man wearing a white tuxedo and carrying a walking stick strolls from one table to another, making small talk. A scene from a movie of the 1940s? No. The year is 2001 and the club is one of many newly opened establishments with old themes that are attracting young, affluent patrons in their twenties. *Many of today's young adults are making successes of clubs that feature the music and atmosphere enjoyed by their grandparents and viewed with contempt by their parents.*

### Topic Sentence 1

Jazz clubs, once the domain of die-hard jazz fans, have emerged as the new place to be seen.

### Topic Sentence 2

Big band music and swing dancing have skipped a generation and found fans among couples in their twenties.

### Topic Sentence 3

Baby boomer parents are experiencing an entertainment generation gap with their children, who are connecting with their grandparents in this new/old entertainment.

---

---

---

How does your conclusion paragraph compare with those provided Review the conclusions that follow each example and compare them with yours. The two will be different, but both efforts should reflect the introduction paragraph and thesis sentence.

### Example A Conclusion

The reinvention of home economics is a positive note in education. Too many of us take for granted that children are receiving instruction in practical skills at home from their parents, but many do not. Knowing how to budget, maintain a home, and keep themselves fed without the fear of food poisoning are skills that are just as important as subjects that are assessed on state skills tests, such as English, mathematics, and science. The bonus, as supporters remind us, is that home economics courses use these skills as well.

### Example B Conclusion

Fad or trend, the reach by young people into the past for their entertainment has had a benefit beyond providing them a link with their older relatives. The renewed interest in big band music, jazz, and swing dancing has also revived the fortunes and record sales of artists who had put their careers aside long ago. Trend spotters view this interest with little surprise, seeing this latest trend as simply further evidence that everything old eventually becomes new again.

# Creating Strategies for Conclusion Content

The effective conclusion, in addition to being well-constructed, places the writing in a useful context. The conclusion should at least end the writing with a clear summary of the key points or highlights of the work, but it should not repeat phrases or sentences from the body or methodically list the details that have appeared in the writing. In addition to offering a summary of the writing, the writer may raise issues that are related to the topic and provide recommendations for exploring the issue further. A conclusion may use only one or two of these approaches, or it may include elements of all three. Straightforward as these tasks may seem, they require quite a bit of skill. The ending should shout "Finale!" but do so in a way that is graceful and informative.

How can you **summarize** without being redundant? Begin at the beginning—with your introduction paragraph. Read the paragraph, underline key words and phrases, distill the ideas into one brief sentence—but do not repeat the thesis sentence.

**Raising related issues** without breaking new ground and confusing your readers can be tricky. The issues must be close enough to serve as examples of the manner in which the current discussion can have further impact, yet they must also stay within the boundaries set by your writing for the topic.

**Providing recommendations for further consideration** may seem to be more suited to academic than everyday writing, but writers often find that they provide unintended recommendations in the course of the writing that later find their way into the conclusion. The recommendations may be direct or implied.

Use the "Consumerism" topic that appeared earlier in this chapter and develop three different conclusion paragraphs. Place emphasis in each introduction on one of the three strategies: summary, raising related issues, or providing recommendations for further consideration.

Write a concluding paragraph that uses the **summary** approach, then compare your attempt to the example below.

_____

_____

_____

## Summary

The disposable nature of our society has made our ownership of any purchase only temporary, at best. The durable black telephones that once meant Bell Telephone are symbolic of a long-gone day, and most of the items that we purchase today will not last long enough to be antiques of the future. Classic cars will continue to be the cars already designated "classic," because few being manufactured today will last the fifty years or more required for the designation. How sad to have become a society of planned obsolescence.

Write a concluding paragraph that uses the **raising related issues** approach, then compare your attempt to the example below.

_____

_____

_____

## Raising Related Issues

Permanence is becoming increasingly rare in all areas of life. The items we purchase fail to last more than a few years. Manufacturers seem to know the exact year of their demise, for they limit service contracts and warranties to a specified time that is usually the useful life of the product. This attitude extends beyond manufactured goods, as society has also developed a disposable mindset toward human relationships. The high rates of divorce, elder abuse, and child endangerment show that the attitude regarding consumer goods is often applied toward other people as well. It is unfortunate that our society would choose to be consistent in so negative a behavior.

Write a concluding paragraph that uses the **providing recommendations** approach, then compare your attempt to the example below.

---

┌─────────────────────────────────────────────────────────┐
│                    ▭▭▭ QUICK TIP ▬▬▶                     │
│                                                         │
│                  ## Select a Strategy                   │
│                                                         │
│ Use the introduction and topic sentences to provide information for │
│ determining which strategy to use in the conclusion. Summarize, raise │
│ related issues, or provide recommendations for further consideration— │
│ select one or use all three approaches in your conclusion. │
│                                                         │
└─────────────────────────────────────────────────────────┘

---

### Providing Recommendations

We have become accustomed to items that break soon after purchase and service contracts that promise only a few years of product functioning. As a result, we actually feel grateful to own an item that gives decent value and has a reasonably useful life span, which we mistakenly view as privileges rather than as our rights as consumers. We should not continue to accept such abuse. Manufacturers who continue to sell poorly made products should be boycotted, and legislation must be passed to guarantee that consumers do not continue to be victims of planned obsolescence. Consumers must raise their expectations and prove to industry that we are not a disposable society.

**SELF-TEST**

Read the following introduction paragraph and topic sentences carefully to obtain a thorough understanding of the writer's direction.

Write three concluding paragraphs, each using one of the three strategies for conclusions: summary, raising related issues, and providing recommendations for further consideration.

Many people in the United States are obese. Walk down the street of any major city, and you will find that most of the passersby will be carrying an extra twenty pounds or more. Visit a public beach, and you will cringe at the amount of loose, glutinous flesh extending above waistbands and beyond the boundaries of swimsuits. This excess flesh is not only unsightly, it is also dangerous to health.

### Topic Sentence 1

The risks of heart attack and stroke increase when a person is twenty pounds or more overweight.

### Topic Sentence 2

Diabetes is more likely to develop in overweight individuals than in those of normal weight.

### Topic Sentence 3

Certain cancers occur more frequently in obese populations than in their slimmer counterparts.

### Summary Conclusion

_____

_____

_____

### Related Issues Conclusion

_____

_____

_____

### Recommendations for Further Consideration Conclusion

_____

_____

_____

**ANSWERS**

Your conclusion paragraphs will probably contain different information from those below, even when you use the same strategy. Compare your paragraphs to the samples and see how closely you used each strategy to develop your conclusion.

### Summary Conclusion

Obesity is a major health issue in the United States, and those who doubt this have only to walk in a major city or on the beach during the summer. The amount of loose flesh hanging out of too-tight clothing is convincing. These people don't realize that they risk suffering early heart attack and stroke, diabetes, and certain cancers, among other indirect ailments. Seeing so many people deliberately placing their health in danger upsets health professionals, who view such disregard as wasteful—wasteful of health and of the lives that will be lost.

### Raising Related Issues Conclusion

Obesity is a major health issue in the United States, but people are not solely responsible for their weight. Some have low metabolism that prevents them from burning sufficient calories, even if they eat low-calorie diets and deprive themselves of foods that are important to their health. Others do not have the money to purchase nutritious food, nor the training to identify the nutritionally best foods. Still others have psychological needs for food, cravings that food satisfies, and they remain overweight for long periods despite participation in behavioral training groups. All of these issues must be confronted if the

United States is to lessen the number of its citizens who are obese.

### Providing Recommendations for Further Consideration Conclusion

Risking death and disability by being obese is not a conscious choice made by most overweight Americans. Some strive to be thinner, while others feel confident that their weight is harmless, for they can point to overweight close relatives or acquaintances who lived long and healthy lives. They fail to take into account the many other obese individuals who are the annual statistics, dead due to heart failure, stroke, diabetes, and cancer, all with obesity as a contributing factor. More education about the link between obesity and serious illness must appear in areas that people of this group see—television, movies, billboards. The ads should be unattractive, to show how being overweight can mean death. Those who will charge that such a campaign amounts to discrimination against the weight-challenged must be shown the data and the sadness and suffering that accompany the data. Obesity does not mean simply enjoying food—it means using food as a weapon to commit suicide.

---

## Conclusions with a Purpose

1. Avoid weak and irrelevant conclusions.
2. Create strong conclusions that reflect the introduction paragraph and topic sentences.
3. Use one of the strategies identified to structure the conclusion.

---

**CHAPTER SELF-TEST**

Following each introduction and related topic sentences, determine which of the three conclusion paragraphs correctly completes the essay. Identify the strategy used in the correct conclusion.

## Essay I

Rock music stars have become more sedate in their personal lives than those of the 1960s and 1970s. No longer do they flaunt their use of illegal drugs. While groupies may continue to exist, their presence is played down in public interviews. The onstage antics that cost groups thousands of dollars in equipment that was smashed and bashed to the delight of fans rarely if ever occur today. Taken in total, rock music has lost its attraction for many listeners who feel betrayed by the maturing of their idols.

## Topic Sentence 1

People who claimed to be rock fans when their chief enjoyment lay in watching stoned singers and drummers try to stay vertical while playing music onstage never truly liked the music.

## Topic Sentence 2

The reports of vast numbers of groupies surrounding each band were inflated, and health scares have dampened the enthusiasm of other would-be groupies.

## Topic Sentence 3

Destroying equipment and running amok onstage was costly and often meant the loss of a favorite instrument.

## Conclusion A

Rock and roll music has steadily lost a following because it is music made by the baby boomers and not Gen X and later generations. The onstage activities and goings-on behind the scenes still hold fascination, but not when they are perpetrated by a group of over-the-hill "wannabes" and "neverweres." The trouble with the rock groups is that they got old.

## Conclusion B

Rock music has grown old, more gracefully to some than to others, but it still has a place in the hearts of many people who are the true fans. Call us baby boomers or call us middle-aged, we are a generation who loved the music and tolerated the antics as being part of the mystique. That is why rock music—

without the groping groupies, bashed guitars, and snake-biting tricks—still draws us to concerts, to hear our music live. The groups have matured, and they have refined their skills, as do true craftsmen. As such, they require an audience whose hearing is fine-tuned to the qualities of the music, not just out for some crash-and-bash.

### Conclusion C

Rock music has lost its attraction among the small group of followers for whom rock meant noise, violence, and sex. It hasn't lost its attraction for us who loved music. What went on at concerts or onstage, aside from the music, had no interest for the die-hard music fans. They really did not know rock music, so how could they support it? People should study and learn a topic before they decide that it is no longer relevant. Who can tell what tomorrow will bring.

**ANSWER**

Conclusion A descends into name-calling and generalizing about the generations in relation to music, but it provides no substantive understanding of the writer's perceptions. Without this understanding, a coherent conclusion cannot be written.

Conclusion C supports the importance of rock music, but the writer gropes for ideas to support the position. The writer should aim for more focused assertions and avoid generalizations that weaken all attempts at producing a valid conclusion.

Conclusion B offers the reader a discussion of related issues that place the main issue in a context. The writer does not defend rock music in a wholesale fashion, but instead educates the reader as to who the true lovers of rock music once were and why they remain lovers of rock music, without all of the drama and destruction. *The strategy used is that of raising related issues.*

### Essay II

Censorship continues to threaten our individual freedoms, despite the growing sophistication of American society. Books, movies, plays, and the Internet have become targets of censors in recent years, and the issue shows little sign of abating. Religion, the media, and the world of art have also experienced attempts to stifle freedom of expression. Such efforts run counter to the rights guaranteed us by the United States Constitution and our justice system.

## Topic Sentence 1

The First Amendment to the U.S. Constitution forbids Congress from enacting laws that would regulate speech or press before publication or punish after publication.

## Topic Sentence 2

The due process clause of the Fourteenth Amendment makes the First Amendment applicable to the states.

## Topic Sentence 3

Court decisions, congressional legislation, and administrative regulations have resolved censorship issues not directly protected by the amendments.

## Conclusion A

Few people have any idea as to just how destructive censorship is to Americans, until they are directly affected. As more of our freedoms are taken from us, we cherish ever more highly those that remain. That is why we must fight censorship and use the defenses that our government has provided us with.

## Conclusion B

Freedom to do what we wish, as long as we don't hurt others, is guaranteed to us by the U.S. Constitution. No one can tell us what to read, watch, or listen to, so the censors should stop trying to do so. Without censorship, this would be a better and more free nation.

## Conclusion C

American citizens must guard carefully the rights they have been guaranteed by the Constitution and the courts. Censorship is a restriction of freedoms promised by the First and Fourteenth

Amendments. Those who would seek to proscribe what we read, listen to, and view are acting in direct opposition to the values that underlie our laws. We do not have to agree with other people's taste in music, movies, books, or art, but we must not place restrictions on them, because each act of censorship is a lessening of freedom for all Americans.

**ANSWER**

Conclusion A refers in general to the defenses against censorship that the Constitution and laws provide, but fails to complete the specific essay suggested by the introduction paragraph and topic sentences. The text suggests that the preceding discussion may have presented a debate regarding the merits of censorship, rather than an examination of the ways in which Americans are protected against censorship.

Conclusion B offers a strong anticensorship stance, but it does not provide a discussion of the safeguards that the Constitution and laws provide. A review of the introduction paragraph, with particular attention to the thesis sentence, exhibits that the focus of the essay is upon these safeguards.

Conclusion C supports the introduction and the thesis sentence with specific references to the amendments discussed and the role played by the courts. The writer does not introduce new issues nor take a combative stance. Rather, the conclusion makes references to the ideas suggested by each of the topic sentences and completes the essay by summing up. *The strategy used is that of summarizing.*

### Essay III

Music and the arts are subjects considered a low priority in many high schools. The emphasis upon standardized test scores as indicators of student success or failure and as yardsticks to measure the success or failure of schools has led administrators to guard strenuously the instruction time in math, English, and science, while neglecting music and art curricula. This alarming trend, which can be observed in elementary, middle, and high schools, is detrimental to the educational development of students and may impede rather than enhance their learning in other subjects.

### Topic Sentence 1

Students in the elementary school grades enjoy learning more when visual and auditory enhancements are used.

### Topic Sentence 2

Middle school students experience the world outside the classroom through graphic imagery and sound and their natural creativity can be enhanced by courses that develop these interests.

### Topic Sentence 3

Most high school students are unsure of their future professions, and a curriculum containing music and art provides additional options to those interested in the creative arts.

## Conclusion A

As long as taxpayers provide the money to run schools and pay the salaries of teachers and administrators, parents should have a say in what their children learn. A lot of famous people have decided on their professions while in high school, and not everyone wants to have a career in mathematics, English, science, history, or foreign languages. We should include more courses in art and music to offer a choice.

## Conclusion B

The arts offer students many opportunities to learn and numerous ways of applying what they learn in their academic subject classrooms. Although standardized tests provide an important measure of school effectiveness and student knowledge, lessons learned to perform well on such tests do not comprise an effective nor a complete education. Young children who enjoy learning will be more eager to learn, adolescents who see some relevance between what they learn in the classroom and what they experience in the outside world will be more receptive to instruction, and older students who are provided with coursework that is diverse and encourages creativity will be more likely to explore further learning options. Rather than decrease the attention to music and other arts in the school curriculum, educators should identify ways of using the arts to enhance learning and to help students to receive the comprehensive education all children deserve.

## Conclusion C

Very little of what goes on in the classroom actually passes for learning in the outside world. Many adults would readily agree with rock singer Bruce Springsteen, who states in one of his songs, "I learned more from a three-minute record than I ever learned in school." The reason is that most schools continue to instruct students as they have been doing for the last hundred years, using memorization and drills rather than innovative thinking. New ideas are ignored by school boards and school administrations because they may mean added expenditures for new textbooks and equipment or additional teachers. Instead of thinking only about money, schools should focus their attention on providing our children with the tools they need to learn and to become productive citizens.

**ANSWER**

Conclusion A provides a series of opinions that, while strong, are not supported by the text of the introduction and the three topic sentences. The rights of taxpayers to select curricula are not indicated in the preceding statements, and the writer does not connect this thought to the sentences that follow. Further, although the writer generalizes about the role that music and art have played in producing famous people, the attention-getting statement stands alone and lacks the development that might make an important point. The final statement appears without basis and functions as a weak statement of opinion that has no apparent connection with the essay.

Conclusion C is a weakly sustained attack on the schools, with support from lyrics written by rock singer Bruce Springsteen, but the paragraph does not conclude the specific essay outlined in the introduction and topic sentences. The words "music" and "the arts" do not appear in the paragraph, nor does the writer indicate that courses in these areas are under discussion. The paragraph ends with a commendable call for strong educational standards, but the specific topic of the essay is avoided completely.

Conclusion B supports the introduction and the thesis sentence with specific references to the positive impact of instruction in music and other arts on students at three specific instructional levels. The writer does not introduce issues not suggested by the topic sentences nor take a combative stance. Rather, the conclusion makes references to the ideas suggested by each of the topic sentences and completes the essay by suggesting recommendations for further consideration. *The strategy used is that of providing recommendations for further consideration.*

# 6 Revising for Greater Understanding

## Objectives

In this chapter you will learn to:

- achieve unity, coherence, and logical development in the final draft

- revise paragraphs to create internal unity and logical development

- create sentences that explicitly state your ideas

One draft is not enough. Experienced writers find that the organization, expression of ideas, focus, and content of anything they write can always be made better, and they will usually read through and revise their work several times before completing a final copy.

Revisions can take several forms, from simple spot revisions to more dramatic global renovation. The revision required depends on the quality of the writing you are working with, and the objectivity you can bring to the work—from the perspective of readers, not your own subjective standpoint as the author.

You must learn to stand outside of the work and see its flaws as well as its good points if you are going to be able to read it as your audience does. If you find that you are too possessive of every word and phrase you write, then the best way to obtain a different perspective is to ask someone else to review it. However, if you ask for such assistance, you must play fair. If your reviewer makes suggestions or points out areas that are unclear, resist the urge to defend your work. You also owe it to them to take any criticism seriously. Keep in mind that if you know the reviewer fairly well, or at least better than later readers might know you, areas that lack clarity in the opinion of your selected reader will be even more confusing to outsiders.

The timid may revise only one sentence at a time, but bold writers must be willing to subject the entire writing to scrutiny. You must be brave enough to make global revisions that will often have great ramifications for your writing, as not only sentences but entire paragraphs may have to be dropped, and shorter paragraphs developed into longer and stronger ones. Paragraph order may change and complete sections be moved. As revisions continue, the key content may underscore new changes, and you may find that you will be led toward different assumptions and conclusions because of the changed content.

Making such radical changes to your writing is much easier if you first place yourself at a distance from the work, by putting the writing aside for several hours or overnight—then approach it as a stranger might. Keep a red or blue pen handy to mark areas in which meaning is unclear, words appear vague, transition (movement from one section to the next) is rough, and other inadequacies exist in unity and organization.

# Creating a Unified and Coherent Final Draft

Writing that is unified, organized in an appropriate pattern, and developed logically conveys a coherent message to readers. Unity depends upon how successfully a writer integrates all elements of the writing, from the development of the thesis statement and topic sentences, through the organization and ordering of paragraphs and the sentences within the paragraphs. Every paragraph must be logically connected to the thesis sentence and to the paragraphs that immediately precede and follow.

The writing must function as a carefully integrated whole, in which each element exists to support and work with every other element. Although a writer may stretch the limits in writing creative nonfiction, most unified writing requires tight organization and should be free of digressions. In seeking to strengthen the unity of your writing, a good rule to follow is to eliminate from the text any discussion and information that is not logically related to the thesis sentence. Ideas that do not work to support your main idea will only serve to detract from the impact of your writing.

A writer may produce five or six strongly written paragraphs that deal accurately with a specific main idea, but the writing will not be unified or coherent if the paragraphs are not placed in an order that effectively carries out the mission of the thesis. The following essay written by a student contains four fully developed paragraphs, but they are not organized in a unified manner. The thesis statement of the essay was: *For true learning to occur, students must recognize the practical value of the subjects they study in school.* The organization of the paragraphs does not provide an effective discussion for the reader. Place the paragraphs into correct order, and explain why your reorganization provides a more effective discussion of the topic.

### Paragraph 1

Schools must emphasize that what they teach to students is useful, not merely a means of fulfilling state mandates or test requirements. Education provides life skills, even if such skills seem to be hidden when presented in the prescribed manner in a classroom setting. Those who remain unconvinced need look only at the occupations that impact on their lives and try to imagine the same people carrying out the same work but without their current levels of understanding of mathematics, language arts, and science skills. They may have received specialized training, but it all started in elementary and secondary school.

### Paragraph 2

Science comes alive to students when teachers reveal that the subject involves more than simply memorizing the periodic table or conversion formulae. The world surrounding students is filled with scientific possibilities. Measuring the pH levels of water in a pool, applying pressure to move a heavy object, mixing ingredients to complete a human or plant food recipe, and numerous other daily activities involve scientific knowledge. When we view natural phenomena, such as animal behaviors that change with the seasons, or weather activity, we make assumptions and decisions that are based upon information learned in a science class.

## Paragraph 3

Unlike studying English, mathematics is usually more understandable even to students who do not have strong language skills. Computations, even in the absence of computers and calculators, are easy to perform, because the language of numbers seems to transcend language barriers. Students profess to understand mathematics, but that enjoyment lessens as higher-level, more significant skills are required. Once students are asked to solve for variables in algebra, they often protest that they will never have to find the value of "y" in real life. Less than a decade later, a teacher might meet the same student who will be calculating how much to pay per yard of carpet or material sold in bulk, and the student might be surprised to be solving for "y" (the price per yard, in this case) all over again. Geometry is also often disparaged by students, who complain that it's useless to figure out area, perimeter, and the like. Once these same students must spend money to install a new floor or pay for someone else to install an expensive fence, geometry skills become valuable. Some students have the same negative feelings about other subjects, such as science.

## Paragraph 4

Students who are exposed to many different subjects gain important tools for dealing with life, and English courses offer them the means of communicating. The study of grammar and punctuation may seem to be a waste of time, and the revision and correction of sentences can appear meaningless, but these are tools that become valuable when clear communication is required. Lengthy novels, drama, and poetry can appear to be exercises in futility, readings meant simply to fulfill requirements, but the ideas and human experiences that appear in literature are also valuable in broadening the worldview of readers and testing their powers of observation. To gain such advantages, students must often overcome their aversion to formal language and take the time to learn vocabulary that may be hard to understand.

On the line in front of each paragraph, write the number, using 1 to 4, to show each paragraph's most logical order:

____Paragraph 1    ____Paragraph 2
____Paragraph 3    ____Paragraph 4

The correct order of the paragraphs is: 4, 3, 2, 1. Reorganized this way, the paragraphs follow a logical progression to express strong support of the thesis sentence and to provide a comprehensive summary of the discussion. If you determined a different order, review the explanations provided below.

The topic sentence of the first paragraph provides a clear reference to the thesis sentence that directly precedes it, before identifying the first subject discussed. The sentences that follow offer direct support for the topic sentence and the assertion that studying English improves communication skills. The final sentence of the first support paragraph provides a segue to the second support paragraph by suggesting that students find English to be a difficult subject that is "hard to understand." The writer opens the next paragraph with a reference to the discussion in the preceding paragraph and uses the opening phrase "Unlike studying English" to provide a clear connection between the two paragraphs. The final sentence of the second support paragraph refers to the negative feelings that students have about mathematics and relates that some students feel the same way about other subjects, "such as science." The sentence concludes the examination of mathematics, then provides a transition to the discussion of the importance of science as a source of life skills. Each of the three preceding support paragraphs discusses a specific subject and provides specific details. In contrast, the paragraph following discusses school subjects in general and provides a summary of the writing to this point as well as raising related issues.

---

◁▭▷ **QUICK TIP** ▬▬▶

## Revise for Meaning

Approach your writing as a reader. To check unity, identify the thesis sentence and be able to explain how each paragraph is logically connected to it.

**SELF-TEST**

Review the following paragraphs and reorganize them to create a well-organized, strongly developed essay. The final essay should open with an introduction paragraph containing a clear thesis, follow with three body paragraphs placed into the most effective order, and end with a concluding paragraph that sums up the discussion, raises related issues, or provides recommendations for further thought.

### Paragraph 1

Manufacturers should reevaluate their relationship with consumers and understand that expensive advertising and exorbitant promises are not the way to reach buyers for their products. People today are price-conscious and willing to forgo the glitz and glamour of television commercials and glossy magazine ads in favor of well-made products that perform as promised. They don't need the advertising if they are being offered good value, but the situation is not going to change soon. The reason that manufacturers will continue to pour billions of dollars annually into creating lures for consumers is that they are afraid that their products do not stand on their own merits.

### Paragraph 2

If manufacturers decreased the extent of their advertising, they would lower marketing costs and could pass the savings on to consumers. Their profit margins could be maintained, but consumers would benefit if the drop in advertising costs became a decrease in the price of the product. Consumers would appreciate such savings, which would be more valuable and tangible than watching overpaid models parade across the television screen in unreal landscapes. Lowered prices might also create product loyalty among consumers and result in repeat purchases, which would further decrease the need for flashy advertising.

### Paragraph 3

The advertising industry in the United States is a multibillion-dollar business that increases the costs of the products we purchase. Consumers are seduced by fancy packaging, expensive television spots, and extensive print coverage—all costly ways to acquaint consumers with the merits of products of all types. Instead of spending extensive amounts of money to advertise their products, manufacturers should concentrate on giving greater value to consumers and lowering the prices for the goods they sell.

## Paragraph 4

Manufacturers should place a greater emphasis upon turning out a good product rather than on producing the glitziest advertising. Consumers spend hard-earned money on items that are designed to self-destruct in a short while, as many do in our disposable economy. The result may seem to be good for manufacturers, who profit when consumers must repeatedly buy replacements for their products, but it is bad for this nation in the long run. If products were made well, they would last longer and the garbage dumps would not fill as quickly. People would also have a greater confidence in what they buy and they would save money that could be spent in other needed areas.

## Paragraph 5

Many products are featured in television commercials that are expensive to produce and often misleading in their claims. Vast scenery and opulent settings provide a context for what may very well be a poorly made product that will give little consumer satisfaction. Commercials show gorgeous models of either sex draped across cars, seated on settees, or eating in restaurants that are being advertised. Celebrities are shown using a product, and viewers subconsciously and mistakenly associate the product with the glamorous and famous figure. The cost of producing these commercials and of the similarly costly print advertising adds to the product price without providing increased durability to the goods.

Indicate, using 1 to 5, the most logical order for these paragraphs:
____Paragraph 1      ____Paragraph 2      ____Paragraph 3
____Paragraph 4      ____Paragraph 5

**ANSWER**

Paragraph 3

Paragraph 5

Paragraph 4

Paragraph 2

Paragraph 1

In reordering the paragraphs, first identify the introduction paragraph with the thesis sentence to determine the main direction of the essay. Then identify the conclusion paragraph, which completes the writing with a general summary and highlights of the writing that appear in the body paragraphs. After placing these two paragraphs in the first and last positions, read the topic sentences of each of the remaining paragraphs to determine their order. Observe the final sentences of each paragraph as well, to note where references are made to the subject of the paragraph immediately following.

# Revising Paragraphs for Logical Development

The coherence and organization of a writing depends upon how skillfully the writer orders the specific ideas to support the thesis and arranges the paragraphs that contain those ideas. Placed in correct order, these paragraphs provide an effective and convincing examination of a topic.

As the example in the preceding section illustrates, the order of the paragraphs is determined by the manner in which the writer builds the discussion point by point and exhibits this order through the topic sentences of each paragraph and the suggested connections that appear in the final sentence of each paragraph. The larger writing depends upon the unity and logical development of each paragraph, which must be coherent, well-developed, and unified. All sentences in a paragraph must relate to the topic sentence, and they must be arranged in an order that logically develops the main idea expressed in the topic sentence of the given paragraph. The idea presented in the topic sentence must be fully discussed, but the writing should not become overloaded with repeated examples. Unnecessary sentences disrupt the unity of a paragraph and the development of the thought it contains, so you must carefully revise to remove all irrelevant or redundant sentences.

Read the following paragraph below (broken into numbered sentences) carefully and decide which sentences disrupt its unity by not providing direct support to the topic sentence. On the lines following each sentence, identify those sentences that are disruptive or irrelevant and explain why they should be eliminated. Revise the paragraph by eliminating the disruptive sentences and providing any transitions that are needed to strengthen the connections among the remaining sentences.

1. Cigarette smoke is harmful both to smokers and to those surrounding them.

   _____

   _____

2. Many people believe that smoking is glamorous and provides them with an air of sophistication.

   _____

   _____

3. For some people the habit is hard to break, even if they know that they are placing the health of those they love in danger.

   _____

   _____

4. Smokers are willing to risk their own increased levels of heart disease, stroke, emphysema, and numerous other ailments.

   _____

   _____

5. When considering the effects on others, they try to not believe that their secondhand smoke is also inflicting harm on the health of their families and coworkers.

   _____

   _____

6.  The habit is too great and the desire too strong for a longtime smoker to easily agree to quit without a strong reason to do so.

_____

_____

7.  I have known family members and friends who have gotten into loud arguments in restaurants when nonsmokers have told them to put out their cigarettes.

_____

_____

8.  Perhaps if they knew that they are weakening the lungs of their children and creating the foundation for future serious health problems for those around them, smokers might find the strength to throw away their enslavers.

_____

_____

The topic sentence indicates that the main idea of the paragraph is to discuss the harmful effects of cigarette smoke both for smokers and for people surrounding them. Only sentences that support this main idea should remain in the paragraph, and sentences that do not speak specifically to this point should be removed. The sentences in italics in the paragraph below may contain valid information, but they do not belong in this specific paragraph because they deviate from the main idea that appears in the topic sentence.

Cigarette smoke is harmful to both smokers and to those surrounding them. *Many people believe that smoking is glamorous and provides them with an air of sophistication. [The paragraph is not concerned with the image of the smoker, only with the effects of the smoke on the smoker and others, so this sentence only detracts from the discussion.]* For some people the habit is hard to break, even if they know that they are placing the health of those they love in danger. Smokers are willing to risk their own increased levels of heart disease, stroke, emphysema, and numerous other ailments.

When considering the effects on others, they try to not believe that their secondhand smoke is also inflicting harm on the health of their families and coworkers. The habit is too great and the desire too strong for a longtime smoker to easily agree to quit without a strong reason to do so. *I have known family members and friends who have gotten into loud arguments in restaurants when nonsmokers have told them to put out their cigarettes.* [*The concern of other restaurant patrons for their own health may have motivated the demands for smokers to stop smoking, but the way in which the sentence is presented makes it disruptive to the unity of the paragraph.*] Perhaps if they knew that they are weakening the lungs of their children and creating the foundation for future serious health problems for those around them, smokers might find the strength to throw away their enslavers.

In addition to containing only information and sentences that speak to the topic sentence, paragraphs must be carefully constructed to show logical thought development throughout. As each paragraph in the writing appears in a specific order, each sentence must also hold a particular place in the paragraph. The support sentences must develop the topic sentence and provide specific details, while the concluding sentence must sum up the paragraph and lead into the paragraph that follows. Any disruption of this order will result in a poorly written and confusing paragraph that will be ineffective to the overall writing.

Rearrange the following sentences to create an effective paragraph. Explain why you chose to organize the sentences in the order you picked.

1. Users can apply keyword search to access items in the collection or browse by series.

2. This release contains over two thousand items related to the writings of Frederick Douglass.

3. As with so many of the American Memory's releases, scholars and the general public alike will welcome this site.

4. On November 15, 2001, the American Memory collection of the Library of Congress announced the online release of the Frederick Douglass Papers.

5. The collection also includes a partial handwritten draft of his third autobiography, *The Life and Times of Frederick Douglass,* and a biography of his wife, Anna Murray Douglass, written by their daughter, Rosetta Douglass Sprague.

6. The release of additional papers is planned to occur in 2003.

7. In addition to writings by Douglass and his family, material from authors Horace Greeley, Lydia Maria Child, Henry Ward Beecher, Ida B. Wells, and others is included in the collection.

_____

_____

_____

The correct order for the sentences is: 4, 2, 5, 7, 1, 3, 6. To create an effective paragraph, you must make certain that each sentence fits in well with all the other sentences in the paragraph. Just as important, each sentence must occupy a specific place in the paragraph that is marked by the clue words and transitions that appear in the sentences that precede and follow.

On November 15, 2001, the American Memory collection of the Library of Congress announced the online release of the Frederick Douglass Papers. This release contains over 2,000 items related to the writings of Frederick Douglass. The collection also includes a partial handwritten draft of his third autobiography,

---

⮂ **QUICK TIP** ⮕

# Build Solid Paragraphs

The paragraphs are the foundation of a writing, so make each a coherent, logically developed unit. Only include sentences that support the topic sentence. Discard all irrelevant sentences or those that disrupt the unity of the paragraph.

*The Life and Times of Frederick Douglass,* and a biography of his wife, Anna Murray Douglass, written by their daughter, Rosetta Douglass Sprague. In addition to writings by Douglass and his family, material from authors Horace Greeley, Lydia Maria Child, Henry Ward Beecher, Ida B. Wells, and others is included in the collection. Users can apply keyword search to access items in the collection or browse by series. As with so many of the American Memory's releases, scholars and the general public alike will welcome this site. The release of additional papers is planned to occur in 2003.

**SELF-TEST**

The body paragraph in this essay is taken from a writing that was created using the following thesis statement: *Preschool-age children should not watch television programs nor see movies that contain violence and abusive sexual activity.* Carefully study the list of sentences and reorganize them to create a paragraph that contains unity and logical development. Eliminate irrelevant and disruptive sentences, and rearrange the remaining sentences within to provide a well-organized, unified discussion. Explain the changes that you make.

1.  Bloody fight scenes, horrifyingly brutal characters, and violent chase scenes appear to be real to younger children, who tend to incorporate such images into their view of the world.

2.  Children have to be given strict moral regulations to guide their lives, or they will become dangers to society.

3.  Violence that is glamorized takes on a twisted appearance of acceptance that can have a negative effect on a child's development of a moral sense.

4.  Preschool-age children are very malleable creatures whose sense of right and wrong is undeveloped and open to significant influence.

5.  Few actions anger me more than seeing young children exposed to inappropriate behaviors.

6.  Similar damage can occur when young children are exposed to graphic sexual activity that contains brutality and abusive behavior.

7.  Viewing violent actions onscreen against which characters appear to be powerless creates terror in young children that they will suffer similar attacks and makes them feel helpless and fearful.

_____

_____

_____

## ANSWERS

The body paragraphs that follow should begin with topic sentences relating directly to the thesis sentence, and the sentences within each body paragraph should provide specific details to directly support the topic sentence. To organize the paragraph in the most effective manner, the writer must first identify the topic sentence, then identify the order in which specific details must be presented in order to create the strongest support for the topic.

The main idea of the overall writing appears in the thesis sentence, which is: *Preschool-age children should not watch television programs nor see movies that contain violence and abusive sexual activity.*

Sentences 2 and 5 may raise valid issues that may be raised later in the writing, but they are not specifically related to the topic sentence of this paragraph. As a result, they must be removed because they disrupt the unity and logical development of the writing.

The order in which the remaining sentences must be organized is: 4, 1, 7, 3, 6. If you proposed a different order, review the italicized explanations in the following paragraphs.

Preschool-age children are very malleable creatures whose sense of right and wrong is undeveloped and open to significant influence. [*This sentence uses the term "Preschool-age children" to create a link to the thesis sentence before embarking on the specific point exam-*

ined in this paragraph, which concerns the negative influence that viewing violent scenes can have on children.] Bloody fight scenes, horrifyingly brutal characters, and violent chase scenes appear to be
real to younger children, who tend to incorporate such images
into their view of the world. [*This sentence emerges from the topic
sentence to provide examples of violence that children might view and to
make a general statement about the effect on the child's worldview of
such screen violence. The two sentences that follow offer more specific
examples of the negative effect that such viewing has on children.*]
Viewing violent actions onscreen against which characters
appear to be powerless creates terror in young children that they
will suffer similar attacks and makes them feel helpless and fearful. [*This sentence deals with the fears that children who watch televised
violence will experience, and the focus is on the immediate personal toll.*]
Violence that is glamorized takes on a twisted appearance of
acceptance that can have a negative effect on a child's development of a moral sense. [*This sentence deals with another aspect, the
glamorizing of violence that can exert more extensive, social damage.*]
Similar damage can occur when young children are exposed to
graphic sexual activity that contains brutality and abusive behavior. [*In the concluding sentence, the writer creates a link to the next
paragraph and topic sentence by using the phrase "similar damage,"
before identifying the next topic of discussion that appears in the thesis
sentence, violent and abusive sexual activity.*]

# Writing Effective Sentences

Good writing depends upon well-developed, well-organized, unified
paragraphs that are made up of effective sentences. To be readable and
effective, sentences depend as much on their content and the way in
which the content is presented as they do upon grammar, usage, punctuation, and other concerns we'll review in chapter 7. Aside from containing interesting information, readable and effective sentences also
exhibit variety in length, pattern, and the manner in which ideas are
connected, either through coordination or subordination.

Vary the length of the sentences in your paragraphs. Reading sentences all of the same length is monotonous and boring, and when readers

become bored with sentences they tune out and fail to pay attention to the important message that may lie beneath the monotony. Compare the two paragraphs below, which provide the same factual information but contain sentences that vary significantly in length and pattern.

The vacation site is a favorite spot for many different types of people. The site is a sleepy beach town. The vacation homes are all on the edge of the water. The rich visit to escape their opulent lifestyles. The middle-class visitors seek to duplicate the experience of being at home. The poor venture to enjoy temporarily a quality of life above their normal level. The houses in the town all look the same. The houses are furnished in a similar manner. Even the rental fees are the same for every house. The attraction of the site is hard to determine. Some visit to experience equality. Some visit to blend in and hide. Some have nowhere else to spend vacation time. Democracy works very well in this town. Everyone leaves feeling satisfied with the time passed. This sleepy beach town is everything each visitor expects it to be.

The sleepy beach town, in which all the homes are on the water, is a favorite vacation site for many different types of people, from the rich seeking escape from their opulent lifestyles to the middle classes hoping to maintain the normalcy of everyday life and the poor daring to enjoy the modest accommodations as luxury for a few days. All visitors share the same experience, because the houses and the furnishings are identical and the rent is the same for all. No one really knows why visitors flock here, although some residents suggest that visitors enjoy the equality of being able to blend in and hide from their everyday lives, but others disparage the site and assert that visitors have no other vacation options. Whatever the truth may be, visitors leave satisfied with the sleepy beach town that makes no promises yet fulfills the needs of every visitor.

Both paragraphs contain the same information, but they differ radically in the way they present it. The brief, simple sentences and lack of sentence variety in the first paragraph create a monotonous effect. In the second paragraph, the sentence patterns are varied, and subordinating conjunctions ("because," "although"), relative pronouns ("that," "whatever"), and coordinating conjunctions ("but," "yet") are used to connect two or three short, simple sentences into longer sentences. The sentence variety created by varying sentence length, subordinating and coordinating ideas, and changing the emphasis that is placed on some ideas in comparison to others creates a more interesting paragraph. Take a closer look at the second version of the paragraph to see how the writer links ideas to enliven the writing and create emphasis.

The sleepy beach town, in which all the homes are on the water, is a favorite vacation site for many different types of people, from the rich seeking to escape from their opulent lifestyles to the middle classes hoping to maintain the normalcy of everyday life and the poor daring to enjoy the modest accommodations as luxury for a few days. [*This opening sentence is unusually long, at sixty-one words, but the use of coordination to connect the first six short sentences that appear in the first version allows the writer to draw the reader into a description of the town and its appeal to all manner of people. Placing this information into one sentence actually makes the words easier to read, and it also shows that the appeal for all three economic levels is equally important to the process. The writer not only coordinates information but also makes parts of the sentence grammatically the same. This parallel structure is created in the three parts by balancing word with word: "the rich seeking to escape . . . , the middle class hoping to maintain . . . , and the poor daring to enjoy . . ."*] All visitors share the same experience, because the houses and the furnishings are identical and the rent is the same for all. [*This sentence uses the subordinating conjunction "because" to place primary emphasis on the first part of the sentence, "All visitors share the same experience." By using the coordinating conjunction "and" to create a compound sentence by joining the two brief clauses "the houses and furnishings are identical" and "the rent is the same for all," the writer signals that the two facts are of equal importance. When the subordinating conjunction "because" is then used to connect this compound sentence to "All visitors share the same experience," the writer makes clear that the similarity of experience is the point to be emphasized in this new sentence, and the additional information regarding the appearance of the houses, the furnishings, and the rent are of less importance.*] No one really knows why visitors flock here, although some residents suggest that visitors enjoy the equality of being able to blend in

---

**━━ QUICK TIP ━━**

# Avoid Sentence Sameness

Maintain reader interest by employing sentences that vary in pattern and length, and that are structured to express clear relationships among ideas. Subordinate and coordinate ideas, create parallel structures, and place phrases and clauses at the beginning, middle, and end.

---

and hide from their everyday lives, but others disparage the site and assert that visitors have no other vacation options. [*The writer effectively places emphasis on the main clause, "No one really knows why visitors flock here," and exhibits the lesser importance of what follows by using "although" to subordinate what residents suggest and the remarks that disparage. Within the subordinated clause, the suggestions made by residents and the disparaging remarks are placed on a equal plane by the writer's use of the coordinating conjunction "but."*] Whatever the truth may be, visitors leave satisfied with the sleepy beach town that makes no promises yet fulfills the needs of every visitor. [*The writer increases reader interest by reversing the manner in which information is emphasized in this sentence, as the subordinated information appears first, preceded by the subordinating conjunction "Whatever," and the main point follows: "visitors leave satisfied with the sleepy beach town that makes no promises yet fulfills the needs of every visitor."*]

**SELF-TEST**

Revise the following paragraph to relieve the monotony created by the current sentences. Vary sentence length and sentence patterns, and use subordination, coordination, and parallel structure to create clarity and to emphasize important ideas.

Few activities are as nerve-racking as waiting for college response letters. The letters usually arrive in late March or early April. Most high school seniors watch the mail nervously. They hope to receive a fat admissions envelope from the college of their choice. They cringe at the thought of receiving a flat, business-size envelope. Parents also become involved. They wait eagerly with their children. Many cannot wait to congratulate their children who receive acceptances. Some prepare to comfort and support children who receive letters of rejection. Others hope to see their children fulfill dreams that were lost to them. Everyone is relieved when those distressing few weeks are over. They are content to resume life, even if the news has been bad.

_____

_____

_____

**ANSWER**

The rewritten paragraph below contains the same information as the original, but the many short sentences have been combined to provide more effective expression of the writer's ideas. Notes in italics explain the changes.

Few activities are as nerve-racking as waiting for college response letters, which usually arrive in late March or early April. [*The use of "which" deemphasizes the information that appears in the second part of the sentence and allows the emphasis to remain on the opening half.*] Most high school seniors watch the mail nervously, hoping to receive a fat admissions envelope from the college of their choice and cringing at the thought of receiving a flat, business-size envelope. [*The connection of the two sentences is made in two ways, through coordination and parallelism. The writer uses parallelism in the use of "hoping" and "cringing" and applies the coordinator "and" to indicate that the activities of "hoping" and "cringing" are of equal importance.*] Parents also become involved and wait eagerly with their children. [*The two sentences are combined by using the conjunction "and" to create the compound verb "become involved and wait."*] Many cannot wait to congratulate their children who receive acceptances, and some prepare to comfort and support children who receive letters of rejection. [*The writer combines the two sentences and uses the coordinating conjunction "and" to indicate that the activities of both the parents whose children receive acceptances and those whose children receive rejections are of equal importance.*] Others hope to see their children fulfill dreams that were lost to them. [*To allow readers to focus attention on the unusual nature of the opinion expressed in this sentence, the writer makes no attempt to combine it with any other sentence.*] Everyone is relieved when those distressing few weeks are over. They are content to resume life, even if the news has been bad. [*The writer reorganizes the first of the final two sentences to deemphasize the importance of the time frame by beginning the sentence with the relative pronoun "when" and to place emphasis on the relief that everyone feels. By using the coordinating conjunction "and" to connect the two sentences, the writer signals that the two thoughts that "Everyone is relieved" and "they are content to resume life" are equally important.*]

---

## Strengthen Every Level of Development in Your Writing

1. Review the order of paragraphs to express your intended message.
2. Create unity and logical development in paragraphs by revising sentence order.
3. Combine sentences for emphasis and sense.

---

**CHAPTER SELF-TEST**

Below is the first draft of an editorial submitted to a local newspaper. Review the writing carefully to determine if the writer has included all of the elements necessary for coherent, well-organized writing—an introduction containing a thesis sentence, body paragraphs beginning with topic sentences supported by specific details, and a conclusion that sums up and highlights key ideas in the writing and raises related issues or makes recommendations. Make revisions to ensure that the paragraphs are correctly ordered, sentences within paragraphs create unity and are developed in a logical manner, and thoughts are combined in a way that correctly creates emphasis and connections. Be prepared to explain the changes you make.

A few birds twitter in the trees. An occasional chipmunk runs through the leaves. At night, a few lonely owls can be heard to occasionally swoop in the air. They dive only to grab an occasional slow-moving field mouse. The vocal environmentalist group claims that this forest land is home to numerous animals. These seventy-five acres are relatively devoid of wildlife. The town council has erred. They are allowing environmentalists to obstruct the planned construction of badly needed low-income housing. That housing could be placed on land that is home to so little wildlife.

The forest is not a popular environment for animals. It lacks a necessary source of water to sustain them. The few herbivores that live in the forest find adequate food. They have to leave what environmentalists have labeled their "safe haven" in order to drink. Once outside the forest, they become prey to other animals. Their numbers lessen. Those who seek to establish a wildlife sanctuary on the seventy-five acres admit the dearth of wildlife. They have suggested importing additional species to increase the numbers of animals living in the forest. They have also suggested importing additional members of the few existing species. They seek to increase the numbers of animals living in the forest. They do not have numbers to support their cause for the land to be designated a sanctuary. They intend to increase them to force the creation of a sanctuary.

The infusion of alien species or numbers of species already existing is illegal. Such infusion can be harmful to the new animal inhabitants. The environmentalists have added rabbits, owls, and chipmunks to the forest from time to time. Many of these have been domesticated pets. Their survival rates plunged once they entered the forest. They are unfamiliar with hunting for themselves. These forest interlopers have starved to death. They have been eaten by other forest inhabitants. Members of the environmental group have faced the town council. They have presented their petitions. Members of the environmental group have produced inflated figures for the wildlife population. They have defended the wisdom of creating a sanctuary. They would allocate nearly an acre to each of the present legal populations of the forest. They are unwilling to allocate any land to the human residents. The humans desperately need the reasonably priced homes that can be built on that land.

Over two hundred working families in this town are too poor to purchase their own homes. They cannot use traditional mortgage sources. The city owns the seventy-five acres. The city can obtain a federal grant. We can give those two hundred families the opportunity. This will change their lives. These are mothers, fathers, grandparents, and children. This is their opportunity to own a home. This is also an opportunity for them to purchase the home at a reasonable loan rate. Their new status as homeowners can have ramifications throughout the community. This can result in a revival of business. It can also result in changes in the public schools that their children attend.

The environment must be preserved. Animals must be kept within reasonable surroundings. They must not be provided with so much space. We cannot maintain a sufficient balance of nature. The number of animals can easily be relocated into a much smaller area within the seventy-five acres. Doing that will leave sufficient room to build the two hundred homes. These homes are badly needed by low-income families. The town council should not cave in to the loudest complainants. The town council should consider each situation on a case-by-case basis. They should weigh the needs of a handful of animals. These animals are housed on what to them is a lavish estate. These needs should be weighed against the needs of two hundred families. These families include nearly four hundred children. Like the animals, they also deserve decent housing.

**ANSWER**

Compare your revision of the essay with the one that appears below, in which the writer has made numerous changes. Short sentences were combined to form longer sentences. The longer sentences were structured to create emphasis on important thoughts and to deemphasize or to subordinate less important or dependent thoughts. Unnecessary words and phrases were eliminated.

A few birds twitter in the trees. An occasional chipmunk runs through the leaves. [*The writer leaves the two brief sentences in the opening for a dramatic effect that captures the reader's attention.*] At night, a few lonely owls swoop in the air, diving only to grab an occasional slow-moving field mouse. [*This sentence is formed by combining two brief sentences and turning one into an adverb clause.*] Although the vocal environmentalist group claims that this forest land is home to numerous animals, these seventy-five acres are relatively devoid of wildlife. [*Two brief sentences are combined to form this sentence, and the writer subordinates the thought in the first sentence by beginning it with the subordinating conjunction "Although" to place emphasis on the second sentence that reveals the lack of wildlife.*] The town council has erred in allowing environmentalists to obstruct the planned construction of badly needed low-income housing on land that is home to so little wildlife. [*Three brief sentences are combined to form this one sentence. The writer places emphasis on the thought that "The town council has erred" by beginning the sentence with this statement, then indicates the lesser emphasis on the remaining two sentences by placing the thoughts contained in them into a prepositional phrase and a clause beginning with the relative pronoun "that," respectively.*]

The forest is not a popular environment for animals, because it lacks a necessary source of water to sustain them. [*Two sentences are combined to create this sentence, and the writer shows that less emphasis should be placed on the second thought by using the subordinating conjunction "because."*] While the few herbivores that live in the forest find adequate food, they have to leave what environmentalists have labeled their "safe haven" in order to drink. [*Two sentences are combined to create this sentence, and by using the subordinating conjunction "While" to begin the sentence, the writer places emphasis on the second part of the sentence that states the herbivores have to leave the safety of the forest in order to drink.*] Once outside the forest, they become prey to other animals and their numbers lessen. [*Two sentences are combined to create this sentence, and the writer joins them with the coordinating conjunction "and" to show that the content of both sentences is of equal importance.*] Those who seek to establish a wildlife sanctuary on the seventy-five acres admit the dearth of wildlife and have suggested importing additional species and additional members of the few existing species to increase the numbers of animals living in the forest. [*Two sentences are combined to create this sentence, and the writer joins them with the coordinating conjunction "and" to show that the content of both sentences is of equal importance.*] Because they do not have numbers to support their cause for the land to be designated a sanctuary, they intend to increase them to force the creation of a sanctuary. [*Two sentences are combined to create this sentence, and the writer places emphasis on the thought in the second sentence by using the subordinating conjunction "Because" to deemphasize the clause.*]

The infusion of alien species or numbers of species already existing is illegal and can be harmful to the new animal inhabitants. [*Two sentences are combined to create this sentence, and the writer eliminates duplication of the subject "infusion" and signals that the two thoughts are of equal emphasis by using the coordinating conjunction "and" to join the two verb phrases "is illegal" and "can be harmful."*] Many of the rabbits, owls, and chipmunks that the environmentalists have added from time to time have been domesticated pets whose survival rate plunged once they entered the forest. [*This sentence is formed by combining three short sentences. The writer emphasizes the illegal actions of the environmentalists who are dumping housepets in the forest by using the relative pronoun "whose" to subordinate the information regarding the survival rate of the pets.*] Unfamiliar with hunting for themselves, these forest interlopers have starved to death or were eaten by the other forest inhabitants. [*Three short sentences are combined to form this sentence. The writer eliminates repetitions, such as the pronoun "they," in favor of using the very descriptive noun "forest interlopers" as the subject. The writer deemphasizes the first thought, that the animals are "Unfamiliar with hunting for themselves," by making it into an opening phrase, and uses the coordinating conjunction "or" to place equal emphasis on the infor-*

*mation that they "have starved to death" or "were eaten."*] When they have faced the town council and presented their petitions, members of the environmental group have produced inflated figures for the wildlife population. [*Three sentences are combined to form this sentence. The writer uses the relative pronoun "When" to lessen the emphasis on the actions of facing the town council and presenting petitions, in order to encourage the reader to focus more strongly on the important information that the group "produced inflated figures for the wildlife population."*] As they have defended the wisdom of creating a sanctuary that would allocate nearly an acre to each of the present legal populations of the forest, they have remained unwilling to allocate any land to the human residents who desperately need the reasonably priced homes that can be built on that land. [*Four sentences are combined to create this sentence. The writer deemphasizes the importance of the environmentalists' defense of creating a sanctuary by using "As" to subordinate the thought, and similarly uses the relative pronoun "that" to deemphasize their desire to allocate one acre or more to each present animal inhabitant. By placing the information that "they have remained unwilling to allocate any land to the human residents" in the main clause, the writer has highlighted the thought for readers.*]

Over two hundred working families in this town are too poor to purchase their own homes using traditional mortgage sources. [*Two sentences are combined to create this sentence. The redundant pronoun reference "they" is eliminated as the writer places the information of the second sentence into an adverbial phrase.*] With the city-owned seventy-five acres and a federal grant, we can give those two hundred families—mothers, fathers, grandparents, and children—an opportunity that will change their lives: the opportunity to own a home and to purchase it at a reasonable loan rate. [*Seven short sentences are combined to form this sentence. Repetitive words, such as "they" and "the city" are edited out, and information from the first two sentences regarding the "city-owned seventy-five acres" and "a federal grant" is joined with the conjunction "and" to give them equal importance. In the same way, the information that appears in the sixth and seventh sentences is joined with the conjunction "and" to place "the opportunity to own a home" and "to purchase it at a reasonable loan rate" in equal importance. Using dashes to set off groups within the families provides emphasis.*] Their new status as homeowners can have ramifications throughout the community and result in a revival of business and a change in the public schools that their children attend. [*Three sentences are combined to create this sentence, in which the writer uses the conjunction "and" to connect the thoughts and to place equal emphasis on the three thoughts from the original sentences.*]

The environment must be preserved, but animals must be kept within reasonable surroundings, not provided with so much space that we cannot maintain a sufficient balance of nature. [*Four sentences are combined to create this sentence. The writer emphasizes the thought that "The environment must be preserved" by making it the main clause, and uses the coordinating conjunction "but" to show that the rest of the information in the sentence is of equal importance.*] The number of animals can easily be relocated into a much smaller area within the seventy-five acres, and that will leave sufficient room to build the two hundred homes that are so badly needed by low-income families. [*Three sentences are combined to create this sentence. The writer places equal emphasis on the thoughts contained in the first two sentences by using the conjunction "and" to connect them, but the notion that the homes "are so badly needed by low-income families" is deemphasized by its placement in the subordinate clause begun with the relative pronoun "that."*] Instead of caving in to the loudest complainants, the town council should consider each situation on a case-by-case basis and weigh the needs of a handful of animals housed on what to them is a lavish estate against the needs of two hundred families, which include nearly four hundred children. [*Six short sentences are combined to form this sentence. The writer uses the conjunction "and" to place equal emphasis on the thoughts "the town council should consider each situation on a case-by-case basis" and "weigh the needs of a handful of animals" and places them in the main clause. The information in the remaining sentences is deemphasized through the use of subordination.*] Like the animals, they also deserve decent housing. [*The final sentence is the same in both versions.*]

# 7 Making Your Writing Flow

In this chapter, you will learn to:

- proofread for greater accuracy in content and expression
- punctuate for meaning
- construct effective sentences

The larger issues of organization, thought development, and unity in writing are vital for good communication, but to make your writing accessible to readers, pay close attention to the seemingly smaller concerns of punctuation, sentence errors, and continuity of thought. The best-thought-out argument and the finest description lose their impact when readers are distracted by inaccuracies, or common grammar and sentence structure errors. Proofread your writing, reading it carefully three, four, or more times, with a red or blue pencil in hand to make corrections. Your reward for such effort will be clearer communication with your readers.

# Proofreading for Accuracy

Only an inexperienced—or inconsiderate—writer would submit a first draft to readers and expect them not to notice or care. No matter how much time you take to write an essay, report, editorial, or letter, one version only is not enough, even if you believe it to be perfect. Every time you write, prepare to read through your work several times to identify errors in content and expression. As most high school and college writing teachers will attest, including the author, who estimates that in her years of teaching she has graded over 50,000 essays, the most common errors are those involving statistics, because even the most meticulous writers transpose numbers, overlook decimal points, and over- or underreport zeroes in citing figures. Errors in the use of proper nouns, such as surnames and names of geographical locations, are the second most frequently identified mistake in writing.

Do not be lulled into a feeling of false security even if you have a sophisticated computer word processing program. Many such programs contain features to alert writers that words are misspelled, and many also identify repeated words, incorrect verb forms, and run-on sentences. Writers can become dependent upon such programs and may become reluctant to take the time to match numbers and names manually. Yet checking your work against original sources is necessary, because no program can determine which numbers are correct and which are incorrect, nor can a word processing program contain all possible proper names.

In the next example, compare the content of a writer's first version of a passage that contains extensive numerical information with the final copy, which has been proofread and corrected several times. The writer's first version of the material follows the final copy. Identify the errors that the writer made in the first draft and underline them.

## Final, Corrected Passage

The existence of U.S. troops serving in Vietnam began in December 1961, with the arrival in Saigon of 400 uniformed army personnel, who were there to operate helicopter companies, not to serve as combat troops. By December 1962, the U.S. government had placed 11,200 military personnel in the country. The number grew to 27,000 in March 1965, when a brigade of U.S. Marines was positioned south of the demilitarized zone at Danang, and U.S. combat strength increased to

200,000 by December of that year. As U.S. leaders made attempts to end the war, troop buildups continued. After U.S. president Lyndon B. Johnson met with Soviet premier Aleksei N. Kosygin in the famous Glassboro (New Jersey) Summit, in an effort to gain Soviet aid in bringing about negotiations with the North Vietnamese, Johnson announced that the U.S. would have 525,000 troops stationed in Vietnam by early 1968. In 1969, U.S. military strength in South Vietnam peaked at 541,000. The already unpopular war began to lose even more supporters as casualties began to increase. In November 1967, the U.S. reported that 15,058 American soldiers had lost their lives in Vietnam since 1961 and 109,527 had been wounded. By the time all U.S. forces were pulled out of Vietnam in April 1975, the deaths would reach 58,022, whose names are now inscribed on the Vietnam Veterans Memorial. Nearly 200,000 would suffer physical wounds, and numerous others psychological wounds. After the cease-fire agreement was signed, 587 prisoners of war, both military and civilian, were released, but the number of personnel unaccounted for, those missing in action (MIA), hovered around 2,500.

## Writer's First Draft

The existence of U.S. troops serving in Vietnam began in December 1961, with the arrival in Saigon of 4000 uniformed army personnel, who were there to operate helicopter companies, not to serve as combat troops. By December 1963, the U.S. government had placed 11,200 military personnel in the country. The number grew to 27,00 in March 1965, when a brigade of U.S. Marines was positioned south of the demilitarized zone at Danang, and U.S. combat strength increased to 200,000 by December of that year. As U.S. leaders made attempts to end the war, troop buildups continued. After U.S. President Lyndon B. Johnson met with Soviet Premier Aleksei N. Kosygin in the famous Glassboro (New Jersey) Summit, in an effort to gain Soviet aid in bringing about negotiations with the North Vietnamese, Johnson announced that the U.S. would have 52,000 troops stationed in Vietnam by early 1966. In 1969, U.S. military strength in South Vietnam peaked at 551,000. The already unpopular war began to lose even more supporters as casualties began to increase. In November 1967, the U.S. reported that 15,850 American soldiers had lost their lives in Vietnam since 1963 and 109,527 had been wounded. By the time all U.S. forces were pulled out of Vietnam in April 1975, the deaths would reach 58,022, whose names are now inscribed on the Vietnam Veterans Memorial. Nearly 200,000 would suffer physical wounds, and numerous others psychological wounds. After the cease-fire agreement was signed, 537 prisoners of war, both military and civilian, were released, but the number of personnel unaccounted for, those missing in action (MIA), hovered around 2,500.

Review the numbers in italics in the next passage and note that the correct figures appear in parentheses following each error. Did you identify all of the errors? If not, which did you miss? Why did you miss them?

The existence of U.S. troops serving in Vietnam began in December 1961, with the arrival in Saigon of *4,000* (400) uniformed army personnel, who were there to operate helicopter companies, not to serve as combat troops. By December *1963* (1962), the U.S. government had placed 11,200 military personnel in the country. The number grew to *27,00* (27,000) in March 1965, when a brigade of U.S. Marines was positioned south of the demilitarized zone at Danang, and U.S. combat strength increased to 200,000 by December of that year. As U.S. leaders made attempts to end the war, troop buildups continued. After U.S. President Lyndon B. Johnson met with Soviet Premier Aleksei N. Kosygin in the famous Glassboro (New Jersey) Summit, in an effort to gain Soviet aid in bringing about negotiations with the North Vietnamese, Johnson announced that the U.S. would have *55,000* (525,000) troops stationed in Vietnam by early *1966* (1968). In 1969, U.S. military strength in South Vietnam peaked at *551,000* (541,000). The already unpopular war began to lose even more supporters as casualties began to increase. In November 1967, the U.S. reported that *15,850* (15,058) American soldiers had lost their lives in Vietnam since *1963* (1961) and 109,527 had been wounded. By the time all U.S. forces were pulled out of Vietnam in April 1975, the casualties would reach 58,022, whose names are now inscribed on the Vietnam Veterans Memorial. Nearly *300,000* (200,000) would suffer physical wounds, and numerous others psychological wounds. After the cease-fire agreement was signed, *537* (587) prisoners of war, both military and civilian, were released, but the number of personnel unaccounted for, those missing in action (MIA), hovered around 2,500.

Numbers are not the only source of frequent errors in writing. Proper names can also be trouble. Compare the content of a writer's first version of a passage that contains extensive citing of Roman names with the final copy that has been proofread and corrected several times. The writer's first version of the material follows the final copy. Identify the errors that the writer made in the first draft and underline them.

## Final, Corrected Passage

In the 1862 translation of *Meditations* by George Long, readers learn what the Roman emperor Marcus Aurelius (A.D. 121–180) claims to have learned about life from numerous people surrounding him, more than from formal schooling. He writes that he learned good moral values and how to control his temper from his grandfather Verus I, and his father taught him to be modest and manly in character. His mother taught him to be pious, beneficent, and abstemious, as well to follow a simple way of life and to avoid the bad habits followed by the rich. The example of his governor taught him to avoid taking sides with either the Parmularius or the Scutarius at the gladiators' fights, to work with his hands, and to keep out of the affairs of others. The teacher Diognetus instructed him to write dialogues and to study philosophy, as well as to hear Bacchius, Tandasis, and Marcianus. At the age of twenty-five, Marcus began intensive study of the precepts of Stoicism under the guidance of Rusticus the Stoic, who also taught him to never be satisfied with only a superficial understanding of a book and to read carefully. Because of Rusticus, Marcus also became acquainted with the works of Epictetus and learned discipline in his interactions with others. Apollonius taught him to concentrate on purposeful activity and to deal effectively with the respect of friends. He learned from Sextus how to retain the respect of others while expressing empathy with them and to express knowledge without being ostentatious. Alexander the Grammarian taught Marcus how to correct others in a helpful, not reproachful, way, while Alexander the Platonic showed him that he should not use "urgent occupations" as an excuse for neglecting the people in his personal life. From Catulus, he learned to listen to even unjust criticism as a source of insight and to always speak well of teachers. His brother Severus impressed on him the importance of loving members of his family and to love truth and justice, equal rights, and freedom of speech. Through Severus, Marcus also learned to know Thrasea, Helvidius, Cato, and Brutus. He learned self-governance from Maximus, as well as to forgive and to remain free from falsehood. He also expresses thankfulness to the gods who guided his education and saved him from wasting his time in reading histories, resolving syllogisms, or studying the heavens, which require the assistance of fate and the gods.

## Writer's First Draft

In the 1862 translation of *Mediations* by George Long, readers learn what the Roman emperor Marcus Aureole (A.D. 121–180) claims to have learned about life from numerous people surrounding him, more than from formal schooling. He writes that he learned good moral values and how to control his temper from his grandfather Virus I, and his father taught him to be modest and manly in character. His mother taught him to be pious, beneficent, and abstemious, as well to follow a simple way of life and to avoid the bad habits followed by the rich. The example of his governor taught him to avoid taking sides with either the Parmularius or the Scrutarius at the gladiators' fights, to work with his hands, and to keep out of the affairs of others. The teacher Dionysus instructed him to write dialogues and to study philosophy, as well as to hear Bacchus, Tandasis, and Marcianus. At the age of twenty-five, Marcellus began intensive study of the precepts of Stoicism under the guidance of Rusticus the Stoic, who also taught him to never be satisfied with only a superficial understanding of a book and to read carefully. Because of Rusticus, Marcus also became acquainted with the works of Epictitus and learned discipline in his interactions with others. Apollonian taught him to concentrate on purposeful activity and to deal effectively with the respect of friends. He learned from Sextus how to retain the respect of others while expressing empathy with them and to express knowledge without being ostentatious. Alexander the Grammarian taught Marcus how to correct others in a helpful, not reproachful, way, while Alexander the Platonic showed him that he should not use "urgent occupations" as an excuse for neglecting the people in his personal life. From Catullus, he learned to listen to even unjust criticism as a source of insight and to always speak well of teachers. His brother Severus impressed on him the importance of loving members of his family and to love truth and justice, equal rights, and freedom of speech. Through Severus, Marcus also learned to know Thrashea, Helvidius, Kato, and Brutus. He learned self-governance from Maximus, as well as to forgive and to remain free from falsehood. He also expresses thankfulness to the gods who guided his education and saved him from wasting his time in reading histories, resolving syllables, or studying the heavens, which require the assistance of fate and the gods.

Review the proper names in italics in the passage below and note that the correct names appear in parentheses following each error. Did you identify all of the errors? If not, which did you miss? Why did you miss them?

In the 1862 translation of *Mediations* (*Meditations*) by George Long, readers learn what the Roman emperor Marcus *Aureole* (Aurelius) (A.D. 121–180) claims to have learned about life from numerous people surrounding him, more than from formal schooling. He writes that he learned good moral values and how to control his temper from his grandfather *Virus* (Verus) I, and his father taught him to be modest and manly in character. His mother taught him to be pious, beneficent, and abstemious, as well to follow a simple way of life and to avoid the bad habits followed by the rich. The example of his governor taught him to avoid taking sides with either the Parmularius or the *Scrutarius* (Scutarius) at the gladiators' fights, to work with his hands, and to keep out of the affairs of others. The teacher *Dionysus* (Diogenetus) instructed him to write dialogues and to study philosophy, as well as to hear *Bacchus* (Bacchius), Tandasis, and Marcianus. At the age of twenty-five, *Marcellus* (Marcus) began study of the precepts of Stoicism under the guidance of Rusticus the Stoic, who also taught him to never be satisfied with only a superficial understanding of a book and to read carefully. Because of Rusticus, Marcus also became acquainted with the works of *Epictitus* (Epictetus) and learned discipline in his interactions with others. *Apollonian* (Apollonius) taught him to concentrate on purposeful activity and to deal effectively with the respect of friends. He learned from Sextus how to retain the respect of others while expressing empathy with them and to express knowledge without being ostentatious. Alexander the Grammarian taught Marcus how to correct others in a helpful, not reproachful, way, while Alexander the Platonic showed him that he should not use "urgent occupations" as an excuse for neglecting the people in his personal life. From *Catullus* (Catulus), he learned to listen to even unjust criticism as a source of insight and to always speak well of teachers. His brother Severus impressed on him the importance of loving members of his family and to love truth and justice, equal rights, and freedom of speech. Through Severus, Marcus also learned to know *Thrashea* (Thrasea), Helvidius, *Kato* (Cato), and Brutus. He learned self-governance from Maximus, as well as to forgive and to remain free from falsehood. He also expresses thankfulness to the gods who guided his education and saved him from wasting his time in reading histories, resolving *syllables* (syllogisms), or studying the heavens, which require the assistance of fate and the gods.

---

**QUICK TIP**

# Read Your Writing First

Proofread your writing several times to eliminate inaccuracies in content and expression. Keep original data and the correct spellings of names, locations, and other proper nouns near at hand.

A writer uses data and names (partial list below) provided by the Winslow Historical Society to compile a history of the first ten years of existence of the town. The passage below relates information about the town founders and their early efforts to create the wholly planned town. Proofread the passage, using the list provided by the Winslow Historical Society as your source of correct data and the correct spelling of names. Identify the writer's errors and rewrite the passage, correcting any errors.

### Date of Town Founding
1893

### Town Founders (as listed in town records)
James Winslow (1854–1899)        Robert Ravens (1845–1914)
James Winslow, Jr. (1874–1950)   Elvira Ravens (1853–1902)
Maria Winslow (1857–1934)        John Quake (1848–1902)

### Land Owned
James Winslow—581 acres          Robert Ravens—145 acres
James Winslow, Jr.—373 acres     John Quake—234 acres

### Financial Worth after Five Years (in 1898 dollars)
James Winslow—$54,670            Robert Ravens—$12,312
James Winslow, Jr.—$44,356       John Quake—$15,234

### Population Changes from 1893 to 1903
1893—pop. 6
1894—pop. 23
1895—pop. 145
1896—pop. 358
1897—pop. 1,344
1898—pop. 1,342
1899—pop. 1,347
1900—pop. 1,455
1901—pop. 867
1902—pop. 554
1903—pop. 145

## Writer's First Draft

The first ten years of existence for the town of Winslow were exciting, as with any new venture. In 1893, three married couples decided to create a wholly planned community, and together they gathered land and money and embarked on their adventure. James Winslow was the largest landowner, with 581 acres, followed by his son James, Jr., with 337 acres, and John Quark and Robert Ravine with 145 acres and 234 acres respectively. During the first five years, the town grew from its founding six citizens to a population of 1,344 in 1898, and the prosperity of its founders grew as well. Stated simply, in 1898 dollars, the six founders were rich. The financial worth of James Winslow was $54,706; of James, Jr., $43,465; of Maria Winslow, $54,670; of Robert Ravine, $13,212; of Elvira Ravens, $12,312; and of John Quark, $15,238. All would watch the fortunes of their little town grow over its first five years, from a dream into a thriving community, but only one of the founders, James Winslow, would live to celebrate the fiftieth anniversary of the founding of the town. The town experienced its largest size of the ten-year period in 1900, when the population zoomed to 1,455 from 1,342 in the previous year. Sadly, however, the population took a drastic dip the following year, to 876. By the end of the ten-year period, the population of Winslow had dropped back to its 1894 figure. At the end of the ten-year period, the town seemed to be in decline; mercifully, two of the founders had died by then and would not have to bear the sorrow of seeing the shrinking of their dream town.

**ANSWER**

Review the corrected passage below, and determine if you found all of the proofreading errors. The errors are placed in italic type in the passage below, and the correct answer follows immediately in parentheses.

If you did not identify all of the errors, consider why you skipped some. Were you impatient? Did you just skim the lists? Did you miss important word cues?

> The first ten years of existence for the town of Winslow were exciting, as with any new venture. In 1893, *three married couples* (two married couples, the son of one, and a male friend) decided to create a wholly planned community, and together they gathered land and money and embarked on their adventure. James Winslow was the largest landowner, with 581 acres, followed by his son James, Jr., with *337* (373) acres, and John *Quark* (Quake) and Robert *Ravine* (Ravens) with *145* (234) acres and *234* (145) acres respectively. During the first five years, the town grew from its founding six citizens to a population of *1,344* (1,342) in 1898, and the prosperity of its founders grew as well. Stated simply, in 1898 dollars, the six founders were rich. The financial worth of James Winslow was *$54,706* ($54,670); of James, Jr., *$43,465* ($44,356); ~~of Maria Winslow, $54,670;~~ of Robert *Ravine* (Ravens), *$13,212* ($12,312); ~~of Elvira Ravens, $12,312;~~ and of John *Quark* (Quake), *$15,238* ($15,234). *All* (All but one) would watch the fortunes of their little town grow over its first five years, from a dream into a thriving community, but only one of the founders, *James Winslow* (James Winslow, Jr.), would live to celebrate the fiftieth anniversary of the founding of the town. The town experienced its largest size of the ten-year period in 1900, when the population zoomed to 1,455 from *1,342* (1,347) in the previous year. Sadly, however, the population took a drastic dip the following year, to *876* (867). By the end of the ten-year period, the population of Winslow had dropped back to its *1894* (1895) figure. At the end of the ten-year period, the town seemed to be in decline; mercifully, *two* (three) of the founders had died by then and would not have to bear the sorrow of seeing the shrinking of their dream town.

# Punctuating for Meaning

Forget all of the rote grammar rules that may have plagued you in the past, and try to use punctuation as a tool to make your writing communicate rather than simply exist. Commas, semicolons, colons, quotation marks, slashes, dashes, and other punctuation marks are tools to make your writing easier to read and more understandable. Rather than the enemy, they are allies in helping you to sort out for readers the thoughts you want to convey. From your past study of grammar, you are familiar with a list of guidelines for using semicolons, colons, quotation marks, slashes, dashes, and other punctuation that you can apply in your writing with confidence. A review of your grammar book should answer any questions you may have about them.

Commas, however, are another story. No matter how many rules governing the use of commas you may have studied, this punctuation mark poses special problems for writers, especially for those who are writing more than classroom essays. Where commas are concerned, there are few hard-and-fast rules.

## Commas

Commas should be used sparingly and only when your writing requires a pause or the segmenting of one part of a sentence from another part. Derived from the Greek word *komma,* which means "to cut" or "to segment," commas play a number of different roles in sentences, and they are vital in producing rhythm, style, and purpose in writing.

Do not become a "comma king" or "comma queen," but do use your ear to guide your writing and to determine when a comma is needed. Read your writing aloud, and you will find that you pause at certain points to create order for your listener; you hesitate, drop the pitch of your voice, and slow down to make certain that the listener hears your message accurately. When others can only read your writing on paper, use commas to give readers the benefit of your pauses and inflections and to prevent your words and thoughts from colliding with each other.

Read the paragraph below and listen for pauses and drops in pitch. Compare your corrected version with the sample following.

Television is a vast wasteland except for such shows as *Law and Order Saturday Night Live Taxi* and *Star Trek* reruns which make the show seem to have been broadcast in new episodes for decades. For the most part other television shows today play to ignorance. Many might argue that *Saturday Night Live* is as guilty of the preceding sins as most other shows when it is not being dull but such critics are taking too limited a viewpoint. *Taxi* might seem to some to be a poor choice in a list of significant programming but I disagree. The show provides an excellent example of an ensemble cast that really works. The characters include Alex the wise older driver Louie the nasty dispatcher and a collection of young hopefuls Bobby Elaine Tony Latka and John as well as the burnt-out Reverend Jim. The television audience could relate to the characters and their problems. Although the inclusion of *Star Trek* in the list requires no justification I must be honest and reveal that I do not watch reruns of the show and I have not enjoyed the episodes that I have seen in the past. To be fair however the quality of the production and the critical acclaim that the show has received over the years require its inclusion. No one may agree with my choices but I am unconcerned because television viewing is a very personal activity. Furthermore while I have offered my choices for the best television programming please believe that I have no intention of taking time to defend these choices against those who might disagree.

---

---

---

Review the following corrected version of the paragraph. Read the passage aloud once again, and note where the pitch of your voice drops and where you pause. If you did not place commas at those points, do so now.

Television is a vast wasteland except for such shows as *Law and Order, Saturday Night Live, Taxi,* and *Star Trek* reruns, which make the show seem to have been broadcast in new episodes for decades. For the most part, other television shows today play to ignorance. Many might argue that *Saturday Night Live* is as guilty of the preceding sins as most other shows when it is not being dull, but such critics are taking too limited a viewpoint. *Taxi* might seem to some to be a poor choice in a list of significant programming, but I disagree. The show provides an excellent example of an ensemble cast that really works. The characters include Alex, the wise older driver, Louie, the nasty dispatcher, and a collection of young hopefuls, Bobby, Elaine, Tony, Latka, and John, as well as the burnt-out Reverend Jim. The television audience could relate to the characters and their problems. Although the inclusion of *Star Trek* in the list requires no justification, I must be honest and reveal that I do not watch reruns of the show, and I have not enjoyed the episodes that I have seen in the past. To be fair, however, the quality of the production and the critical acclaim that the show has received over the years require its inclusion. No one may agree with my choices, but I am unconcerned because television viewing is a very personal activity. Furthermore, while I have offered my choices for the best television programming, please believe that I have no intention of taking time to defend these choices against those who might disagree.

The second version of the passage, with commas placed to create rhythm and order, is easier to comprehend.

Commas are used in specific situations. Although an intensive review of grammar is not among the purposes of this book, the importance of commas in creating organization, rhythm, and order demands a review of their uses here.

1. Use commas to separate three or more items in a series. Although several newspaper stylebooks eliminate the comma before the last item in the series, you have to decide on a case-by-case basis whether or not to do so. In some situations, omitting the comma at that point may create confusion.

   The outdoor market sells the freshest tomatoes, apples, lettuce, and peaches in the area.

   The preceding example allows the writer the option of including the comma before the last item in the series, but a difference in meaning occurs in the following sentence when the comma is omitted.

   The restaurant offers a limited menu of coffee, juice, waffles, pancakes, sausage, bacon, and eggs.

The restaurant offers a limited menu of coffee, juice, waffles, pancakes, ham, bacon and eggs. [*Omitting the comma after "bacon" suggests that it is commonly offered on the menu as one unit with eggs.*]

2. Use commas after introductory elements (words, expressions, phrases, clauses). Most introductory elements function as adverbs to tell when, where, why, how, or under what conditions the main action of the sentence took place. The comma completes the introduction and signals the beginning of the main part of the sentence.

Walking slowly to the front of the room, the teacher smiled at the students, who waited expectantly for her surprise.

3. Use a comma and a coordinating conjunction to separate the parts of a compound sentence. When a coordinating conjunction (and, but, or, nor, for, so yet) is used to join two independent clauses, use a comma before the conjunction to tell readers that one independent clause has ended and that another will begin. If you read compound sentences aloud, you will find that you pause at the end of the first independent clause, where you should place the comma.

People who ban books seek to impose their values and beliefs on others, but they refuse to keep their minds open to the ideas and beliefs of others.

4. Use commas to set off nonrestrictive words, phrases, and clauses. A nonrestrictive element is a word or group of words that can be removed from the sentence without changing the essential meaning. To determine if an element is nonrestrictive, mentally eliminate it from the sentence and decide if the meaning of the sentence remains clear. If the meaning changes significantly, then eliminate the commas, because the material is restrictive. Note in the preceding example that the modifying phrase "who ban books" is restrictive. If it were removed from the sentence, the intent and meaning would be lost.

Few people aside from the occasional visitor have seen the director of the town library smile.

---

╔═══════════════════════════════════════════════╗

⊏══▶ **QUICK TIP** ▬▬▶

# Use Commas Sparingly

Commas should be used to provide pauses, to create order, and to set off nonrestrictive (nonessential) information. Review your writing to avoid overusing commas.

╚═══════════════════════════════════════════════╝

Few people, aside from the occasional visitor, have seen the director of the town library smile.

5. Use commas to set off a nonrestrictive appositive. An appositive serves to rename a noun or pronoun located nearby. Appositives that are not essential to what they name are nonrestrictive and should be set off with commas.

The young man in the first seat of the first row, Ted, will compete in the free-throw competition. [*Ted has already been clearly identified by his position in the room, so his name becomes unnecessary in the sentence.*]

**SELF-TEST**

Review the passage below that appeared as an example on page 168. The areas in which commas were placed to correct the passage are underlined and numbered. Identify why commas are needed at each point and place your answer on the lines following the passage.

Television is a vast wasteland except for such shows as <u>*Law and Order, Saturday Night Live, Taxi,*</u> (1) and *Star Trek* reruns<u>, which make the show seem to have been broadcast in new episodes for decades.</u> (2) <u>For the most part,</u> (3) other television shows today play to ignorance. Many might argue that *Saturday Night Live* is as guilty of the preceding sins as most other shows when it is not being dull<u>, but such critics are taking too limited a viewpoint.</u> (4) *Taxi* might seem to some to be a poor choice in a list of significant programming<u>, but I disagree.</u> (5) The show provides an excellent example of an ensemble cast that really works, from

Alex, the wise older driver, (6) to Louie, the nasty dispatcher, (7) and a collection of young hopefuls, Bobby, Elaine, Tony, Latka, (8) and John, as well as the burnt-out Reverend Jim. (9) Although the inclusion of *Star Trek* in the list requires no justification, (10) I must be honest and reveal that I do not watch reruns of the show, and I have not enjoyed the episodes that I have seen in the past. (11) To be fair, (12) however, (13) the quality of the production and the critical acclaim that the show has received over the years require its inclusion. No one may agree with my choices, but I am unconcerned because television viewing is a very personal activity. (14) Furthermore, (15) while I have offered my choices for the best television programming, (16) please believe that I have no intention of taking time to defend these choices against those who might disagree.

1. _____

2. _____

3. _____

4. _____

5. _____

6. _____

7. _____

8. _____

9. _____

10. _____

11. _____

12. _____

13. _____

14. _____

15. _____

16. _____

1. list of items in a series

2. nonrestrictive adjective clause

3. introductory phrase

4. with coordinating conjunction to form a compound sentence

5. with coordinating conjunction to form a compound sentence

6. appositive set off by two commas

7. appositive set off by two commas

8. before nonrestrictive appositive (first comma), and items in a series

9. nonrestrictive phrase

10. introductory clause

11. with coordinating conjunction to form a compound sentence

12. introductory phrase

13. nonrestrictive element

14. with coordinating conjunction to form a compound sentence

15. introductory element

16. nonrestrictive clause

# Constructing Effective Sentences

Well-written sentences act as showcases for your ideas. More than a mere grammatical structure, each sentence should function as an important facet of the structure of the paragraph in which it appears, in the same way that each paragraph serves as a building block for the structure of the overall writing. The form of sentences is integral to conveying meaning.

## Short or Long

The subject influences the length of the sentences used in carrying out the mission of a writing. Explanations of an impersonal, technical, or professional nature suggest that the writer create a businesslike mood through the use of short, simple, to-the-point sentences, while meditative, descriptive, editorial, and similar writings are often better expressed in longer, more detailed sentences.

> The market closed 15 points higher today. Traders credit a late afternoon rally in tech stocks.

> The stock market closed 15 points higher today, and traders credit a late afternoon rally in tech stocks for the gain.

These sentences show how concise expression more effectively conveys the information in reporting a business transaction than the compound sentence that is formed by using a comma and a coordinating conjunction to combine the two brief sentences. The writer of the first version believes that the information in each statement of fact is important and deserves its own sentence. Furthermore, the conciseness of expression in each sentence projects a businesslike image.

In contrast, using concise sentences to write descriptions, opinions, or the like might be disruptive to the reader, because the accumulation of such sentences might create a choppy or disjointed style. In the following example, compare the use of concise sentences in one version with the longer sentences in which ideas are coordinated and subordinated in the second version to express a viewpoint.

> The spotted owl is on the endangered species list. Efforts should be made to stop logging in forests in which spotted owls live. Logging operations in areas where the spotted owl lives is harmful. The XYZ Timber Company has plans to begin felling timber in the state forest. Spotted owls have been observed there. The plans of the XYZ Timber Company must be halted.

> The plans of the XYZ Timber Company to fell trees in the state forest must be halted to prevent harm to the spotted owls, an endangered species reported by observers to be inhabitants of the forest.

In the first version, the information is presented in a series of brief sentences, each containing a portion of the information that the writer considers to be important in ensuring the safety of the spotted owl. The more important, generalized call for attention to the issue is obscured by the data provided about the imminent plans of a specific company to fell trees in a particular habitat of the spotted owl. The writer must be concerned with style in eliminating the choppy, staccato expression of the ideas in the first version, yet also emphasize the main idea of the sentence, which is to stop the logging company's plans to fell trees at a specific site. To make the point effectively, the sentence must open with the statement of concern and give only such data as needed to set a context.

## Variety in Expression

Word order and the way you begin and end sentences also influence how effectively you convey your message. The most straightforward sentence pattern is one that begins with the subject, followed by the verb and an object, each with its modifiers.

> The computer industry exerts a great influence in the United States. Computers perform many tasks in business and industry. Instruction in computer skills is also popular in elementary and secondary schools. Most businesses are computerized. Many human workers have lost their jobs because of computers. Retraining in a technical field is one inevitability for many people.

As the example shows, however, the straightforward approach becomes monotonous, and writing made up only of sentences in this pattern will lose readers before they grasp the writer's point. Combining the sentences to create all compound or all complex sentences will not improve the writing—it will only provide a different type of monotony. The proper solution to this problem is to vary the form of your sentences throughout the writing.

One way you can add life to your writing is to invert select sentences in a paragraph. An inverted sentence deviates from the subject-verb-object pattern by moving the subject to the end of the sentence. In writing inverted sentences, make certain that the resulting sentence makes sense and fits the flow of your writing, because many inverted sentences have a stilted quality.

Two heavy gold earrings were dangling from each of her ears and shining brightly in the harsh light of the lamp.

Inverted form: Dangling from each of her ears and shining brightly in the harsh light of the lamp were two heavy gold earrings.

The subject of the sentence in the above example, "two heavy gold earrings," appears at the end when the sentence is rewritten into inverted form, and the attention of readers is focused on the appearance of the earrings "dangling" and "shining."

A second way in which you can introduce variety into your writing is to use a range of sentence openings in each paragraph. Write some of your sentences in the straightforward pattern of subject-verb-object, while revising others to begin with introductory words, phrases, or clauses inserted directly before the subject. Most often, such introductory elements are adverbs that appear as modifiers in the middle or end of the sentence, and they can be relocated to the beginning without detracting from the meaning.

We ran through the alleys to our home as quickly as we could.

Introductory phrase: As quickly as we could, we ran through the alleys to our home.

In the first version, the writer relates an action in a straightforward fashion, placing less attention on the urgency with which the subject ran home. By rewriting the sentence to begin with the introductory phrase "As quickly as we could," the writer changes the focus and conveys the haste and urgency that characterized the run home.

The computer industry exerts a great influence in the United States. [*This simple sentence provides an effective and emphatic statement that should remain unencumbered by additional clauses.*] Computers perform many tasks in business and industry, and instruction in computer skills is also popular in elementary and secondary schools. [*This compound sentence is more effective than the two simple sentences that have been combined to create it, because the two thoughts regarding the popularity of computers are closely linked. The result is a more powerful expression regarding the importance of computers in contemporary society.*] Because most businesses are computerized, many human workers have lost their jobs ~~because of computers.~~ [*This complex sentence takes two simple sentences in which events are presented as independent of each other and combines them into a sentence in which one thought is subordinated or made dependent upon the other thought.*] Retraining in a technical field is one inevitability for many people. [*This simple sentence provides a dramatic closing to the paragraph.*]

The writer of the revision above has taken six sentences written in the straightforward subject-verb-object pattern and recast them into a paragraph that contains two of the original sentences, one compound sentence, and one complex sentence. The different sentence structures provide readers with variety in the rhythm of the writing and increase interest in the subject.

## Emphasis of Ideas

A writer must tell readers where the special emphasis lies in a writing, because readers who are left to decide for themselves what is important will quite likely misread the writer's intentions. Effective sentences alert readers to which ideas are important, and they do so through a combination of strategic placement and careful arrangement of key ideas. If you want readers to remember specific information, place it at the beginning or the end of a sentence. When you place key information in the middle of a sentence, you commit it to obscurity, because readers are too busy moving from the previous sentence into the opening of the present sentence, then moving from the end of the present sentence into the next idea. The middle is often ignored.

> When we looked at her record we found that she is a felon with a long prison record, but she wants to become a public school teacher.

The information at the beginning and the end of this sentence is not as dramatic nor as important as that of the middle section. The placement in the middle of the information "she is a felon with a long prison record" makes the statement much less emphatic than if it appeared at the beginning or the end. Consider how the emphasis shifts when the ideas are reorganized in the following version, with the most important information placed at the end of the sentence.

> She wants to become a public school teacher, but when we looked at her record we found that she is a felon with a long prison record.

You can also place emphasis on the ideas that you want readers to find significant by arranging them in a dramatic manner of increasing importance. Creating a climactic order of your ideas requires a sequencing of details, through which you lead the reader from the least important item to the most important, beginning with the least powerful verb or image and ending with the most powerful.

> Tenants in this housing complex have been tortured by a lack of heat, overcharged by the landlord, awakened at all hours by banging pipes, and plagued by rats and cockroaches.

The example contains several powerful images, but the order is not consistent and the reader is deprived of a dramatic buildup to emphasize the problem. In the following revision, the writer arranges the ideas in climactic order to make the sentence more effective and the expression of ideas stronger.

> Tenants in the housing complex have been overcharged by the landlord, awakened at all hours by banging pipes, *tortured* by a lack of heat, and *plagued* by rats and cockroaches.

---

**◁▭ QUICK TIP ▰▶**

# Avoid Boring Sentences

Effective sentences are interesting sentences that convey the writer's message through variations in length, structure, and emphasis. You cannot make your point effectively if readers stop reading what you write because it is boring.

The verbs "tortured" and "invaded" are both powerful, but the increased intensity of the images created determines that one precede the other.

The following passage does not convey effectively the message intended by the writer, because it is composed of ineffective sentences. Revise the sentences to create variety in their length, structure, and emphasis of main ideas. Combine sentences as needed, and eliminate excess words that become repetitive when two or more sentences are combined into one.

Student math majors often sneered at the English majors. English majors were considered somewhat less respectable. They read books. Their reading was largely fiction. Math majors performed more practical tasks. They proved theorems. They solved mathematical problems. They were able to show application of what they learned. English majors discussed thoughts. Thoughts are not tangible. Some students entered both worlds. They were people without a country. Neither major claimed them completely. Many felt out of place among people of either major. Some students preferred their odd status as dual majors. They were truly happy. They lived in a world of their own making. They enjoyed the intense discussions of literature. They enjoyed the satisfactions of mathematical problem solving.

_____

_____

_____

To revise the paragraph and create effective sentences, combine many of the short sentences to create compound or complex sentences. You might also invert sentences, modify the way sentences begin, and change the order of ideas to create more emphasis on main ideas.

## Respect Your Readers

1. Read your writing several times to identify errors in grammar, usage, and expression.
2. Use punctuation to enhance your writing style.
3. Create effective sentences by varying form and combining creatively.

A writer used information (see boxed text) and other research to create the first writing draft in the following self-test. Proofread the passage carefully. Identify the writer's errors in content, use of commas, and sentence formation, then incorporate all of your corrections.

## Afghanistan Facts in Brief

| | |
|---|---|
| **Capital city** | Kabul |
| **Official languages** | Pashto and Dari |
| **Borders** | North: Turkmenistan, Uzbekistan, Tajikistan; Northeast: China; East & South: Pakistan; West: Iran |
| **Geographical area** | 251,773 sq. mi. |
| **Greatest distances** | E/W: 820 mi.; N/S: 630 mi. |
| **Elevations** | Highest: Nowshak, 24,557 ft. above sea level Lowest: Sistan Basi, 1,640 ft. above sea level |
| **Population** | 1979: 13,051,358 2002: 24,977,000; Density: 99 per sq. mi. |
| **Chief products** | Agriculture: wheat, Karakul skins, barley, corn, vegetables, mutton, nuts, rice, wool, cotton, animal hides; Manufacturing: cement, rugs, processed foods, shoes, textiles; Mining: lapis lazuli; natural gas, coal |

## Writer's First Draft

The events of September 11, 2001, have led many citizens of the United States to seek information about Afghanistan. It is a nation that formerly held little interest. They have consulted atlases. They have searched online. Americans have been disappointed in what they have found. The country is, in general, not very interesting to the creators of travel and information guides; yet it is a land rich in history and culture, waiting to be discovered.

Afghanistan is a nation in southwestern Asia. It is one of the world's least developed countries. The capital city is Kabul. It is the largest city. The size of Afghanistan is 251,673 square miles. The country has 99 people per square mile. The greatest distance from east to west in the country is 630 miles. The greatest distance from north to south in the country is 820 miles. It is a country of great mountains, scorching deserts, fertile valleys, and rolling plains. The highest mountain is Noshwak. It is 24,557 feet above sea level. The lowest point in the country is the Sistine Basin. It is 1,640 feet above sea level. Afghanistan does not have a seacoast. The country is bordered by Turkmanistan, Uzbekistan, and Tajikastan on the north, China on the far northeast, Pakistan on the west and south, and Iran on the east. Afghanistan has about 11,700 miles of roads. However, most paved roads were heavily damaged during the war with the Soviet Union and made unusable. The war with the Soviet Union took place in the 1980s. The country has no railroads.

The population in 1979 was 13,051,385. The estimated population for 2002 is 24,867,000. Eighty percent of the residents live in rural areas. Most of Afghanistan's people fifteen years of age or older cannot read and write. The law requires all children from seven to fifteen years old to go to school. However, many of these children cannot attend school. The country does not have enough schools or teachers. This lack of educational facilities is due largely to the upheaval caused by the past two decades of war. Folklore, folk songs, and folk dances play an important part in Afghan life. They enable the people to pass their values and traditions on from one generation to the next.

About 85 percent of all Afghan workers earn their living in agriculture. Wheat is the chief crop of Afghanistan. Other crops include barley, corn, cotton, fruits, nuts, rice, sugar beets, and vegetables. The chief livestock products are dairy items, mutton, wool, animal hides, and the skins of Karakul sheep. Afghanistan has relatively little industry. A few mills produce textiles. Small factories turn out such products as cement, matches, and processed foods. Skilled craftworkers in their homes or small shops make gold and silver jewelry, leather goods, rugs, and other handicraft items.

Afghanistan is rich in minerals. Most of the deposits are largely undeveloped. In the 1960s, large deposits of natural gas were discovered in Afghanistan. The production of natural gas has become an important part of the nation's economy. Afghanistan also produces some coal, copper, gold, and salt. The country has huge deposits of iron ore. They lie in a remote part of the country. They remain largely undeveloped. Afghanistan is the world's leading producer of diamonds. Other valuable stones mined in the country include amethysts and rubies.

Afghanistan has about twenty ethnic groups. Most of the groups have their own language and cultural pattern. Most of the ethnic groups consist of several tribes. Many of the tribes speak their own dialect. Many Afghans feel greater loyalty to their ethnic group or tribe than to their country. Their religion also influences most other aspects of life. Almost every Afghan village or seminomadic group has a religious leader called a mullah. Mullahs have great influence in their communities. They interpret Islamic law and educate the young.

Afghanistan has had a long and troubled history. In early days, Persians, Greeks, Mongols, and many other peoples conquered the region. In modern times, Afghanistan has suffered from foreign interference. The main sources of interference have come from the United Kingdom and from the Soviet Union. This interference existed from 1922 to 1991. The Soviets sought to occupy Afghanistan in a war that lasted from 1979 to 1989. The Soviets left in 1989. Afghanistan has been torn by bitter struggles for power. The Soviets retreated from Afghanistan in 1989. They put a Communist government in place. In 1992, a coalition of forces overthrew this Communist government. Since then, Afghanistan has had difficulty establishing a permanent and stable government. There has been competition among rival factions. Instead, the country has had several interim (acting) governments. They were made up of coalitions of the factions. By the late 1990s, one of the factions had taken control of most of Afghanistan, including Kabul. This was a conservative Islamic group called the Taliban. The Taliban set up a Council of Ministers to rule the country.

---

---

---

**ANSWER**

The revised passage below contains corrections of errors in the information taken from the chart, as well as revisions to the expression of ideas. The incorrect data is in italics and the correct information is placed directly following within parentheses. The rewritten version combines many of the short, simple sentences into longer, more effective sentences in which less important ideas are subordinated to main ideas. Repeated ideas, subjects, and other information have been removed.

The events of September 11, 2001, have led many citizens of the United States to seek information about Afghanistan, a nation that formerly held little interest for them. Americans have consulted atlases and searched for information online, but many have been disappointed in what they have found. Afghanistan is not, in general, very interesting to the creators of travel and information guides; yet it is a land rich in history and culture, waiting to be discovered.

One of the world's least developed countries, Afghanistan is located in southwestern Asia. Kabul, the capital city, is also its largest. Rather sparsely inhabited, the nation has a population density of only 99 people per square mile. Afghanistan comprises *251,673* (251,773) square miles, and the greatest distance from east to west in the country is *630* (820) miles and from north to south *820* (630) miles. It is a country of great topological contrasts, containing high mountains, scorching deserts, fertile valleys, and rolling plains. The highest mountain is *Noshwak* (Nowshak), rising 24,557 feet above sea level, and the lowest point in the country is the *Sistine* (Sistan) Basin, 1,640 feet above sea level. Afghanistan is bordered by *Turkmanistan* (Turkmenistan), Uzbekistan, and *Tajikastan* (Tajikistan) on the north, China on the far northeast, Pakistan on the *west* (east) and south, and Iran on the *east* (west). Although Afghanistan has about 11,700 miles of roads, it has no railroads. Moreover, most paved roads were heavily damaged and made unusable in the 1980s during the war with the Soviet Union.

The population of Afghanistan has nearly doubled in the last two decades, from *13,051,385* (13,051,358) in 1979 to an estimated population of *24,867,000* (24,977,000) in 2002. Eighty percent of the residents live in rural areas, and most of the people fifteen years of age or older cannot read and write. Although the law requires all children from seven to fifteen years old to go to school, many of these children cannot. The country does not have enough schools or teachers, due largely to the upheaval caused by the past two decades of war. In place of formal schooling, folklore, folk songs, and folk dances play an important part in Afghan life and enable the people to pass their values and traditions on from one generation to the next.

About 85 percent of all Afghan workers earn their living in agriculture. Wheat is the chief crop of Afghanistan, and other crops include barley, corn, cotton, fruits, nuts, rice, sugar beets, and vegetables. The chief livestock products are dairy items, mutton, wool, animal hides, and the skins of Karakul sheep. Afghanistan has relatively little industry, but a few mills produce textiles, and small factories turn out such products as cement, matches, and processed foods, while skilled craftworkers make gold and silver jewelry, leather goods, rugs, and other handicraft items in their homes or small shops.

Afghanistan is rich in minerals, but most of the deposits are largely undeveloped. In the 1960s, large deposits of natural gas were discovered in Afghanistan, and the production of natural gas has become an important part of the nation's economy. The country has huge deposits of iron ore, which lie in a remote region and remain largely undeveloped. Afghanistan is the world's leading producer of *diamonds* (lapis lazuli), and other valuable stones mined in the country include amethysts and rubies.

The nation lacks unity because of the diverse languages and cultural patterns that are inherent to the approximately twenty ethnic groups that make up society in Afghanistan. Most of the ethnic groups consist of several tribes, each with their own dialect, and many Afghans feel greater loyalty to their ethnic group or tribe than to their country. Religion also influences most aspects of life. Afghan villages and groups have religious leaders called mullahs, who have great influence in their communities, in part because they interpret Islamic law and educate the young.

The history of Afghanistan is long and troubled, from early conquests by the Persians, Greeks, Mongols, and others, to modern times, in which the main sources of foreign interference have come from the United Kingdom and the Soviet Union. The Soviets left in 1989, after putting in place a Communist government. Afghanistan was torn by bitter struggles for power, and in 1992 a coalition of forces overthrew this Communist government. Since then, competition among rival factions has continued, and Afghanistan has had difficulty establishing a permanent and stable government. By the late 1990s, the conservative Islamic group the Taliban, one of the factions, had taken control of most of Afghanistan, including Kabul, and set up a Council of Ministers to rule the country.

# __8__ Polishing Your Prose

## Objectives

In this chapter, you will learn to:

- employ accurate and specific terms
- use active rather than passive voice
- avoid bias in writing

Write as if you were the reader, and use language that is appropriate for your subject and meets the needs of your audience. Do not believe mistakenly that longer words, flowery phrases, and highly technical terms will impress readers favorably. Jargon, pretentious language, and euphemisms, as well as slang, regionalisms, and other deviations from standard English, have their place, but that place is most likely not in your writing. Puffed-up language designed only to impress readers with your knowledge will fail to keep them reading. Nonstandard English, when used routinely and not just to make a point, reflects badly on your language skills and leads readers to question your abilities and the extent of your knowledge. Sentences that use the passive rather than the active voice slow the writing and fail to inform readers immediately regarding who or what is performing an action. Bias-laden language is insulting to members of the group pinpointed and to everyone who disdains prejudice. After you have gathered your ideas and organized them in a meaningful structure, review your language choices. Good ideas require the right words, so polish your prose and take an active role in your writing by selecting the best words for your subject.

# Using Specific Language

Good communication requires the use of **precise diction** and **specific verbs** to convey the most accurate and detailed information, whether you are writing an essay, a research paper, a business report, or a letter. Writing that contains vague or imprecise nouns, verbs, or modifiers communicates only generalizations to readers, who are then forced to interpret your intention and meaning.

> *Many* will attend *the function,* and I expect that *many* of your members will be present.
>
> *Three hundred people* will attend *the Holiday Dinner Dance,* and I expect that at least *fifty* of your members will be present.

In this example, the writer of the first sentence provides readers with no boundaries and too little actual information to make the sentence of much value. In contrast, by including in the second sentence the specific number of people, the actual name of the function, and the number of members expected to be present, the writer clearly communicates an intention.

**Adverbs** and **adjectives** should also be judiciously chosen and used as they are needed to provide important information in your writing. Vague, generalized modifiers just provide word clutter in a sentence, and, if overused, they can detract from the information that you seek to emphasize. Avoid the temptation to attach one or more adverbs to every verb; instead, learn to enjoy and to appreciate the power of simple statements. Most readers find that an accumulation of adverbs detracts from the strength of a verb, so select modifiers carefully. The addition of adverbs such as "mournfully," "hopefully," and "sadly" reflects more on the writer's perceptions and opinions than it enriches the reader's experience. Writing is weakened even further when writers attach very general, meaningless adverbs, in a mistaken effort to strengthen weak expression. The following example exhibits the way in which a too general or inaccurate adverb actually detracts from the meaning.

> Professor Armons wrote poorly on the role played by women in combat during the American Revolutionary War.

What is the writer's specific opinion of Professor Armons's writing on the subject? Was the writing inadequately researched? Was the expression of information awkward or disorganized? Did the professor fail to excite the interest of readers? To be more effective, and more valuable, in its assessment, the writing should specify the problem rather than generalize, as the use of the adverb "poorly" can only hint. Read the following revised version of this example.

> Professor Armons failed to provide an in-depth look at the specific accomplishments of women in his account of the role they played during the American Revolutionary War.

Adjectives also pose problems for writers, many of whom substitute general or vague descriptive terms for the details that would create a clearer image for readers. Instead of referring to a building as being "dilapidated," specify the damage and neglect that leads you to describe it as such. Keep in mind that your readers will have had diverse experiences and that the term "dilapidated" may only bring to mind a building that needs to be painted. Other readers might see the term and conjure up an image of cracked windows, a leaking roof, and severe structural damage. To make your meaning clear, include more information in the form of specific details to explain the adjectives. Most adjectives leave significant room for reader interpretation, and that interpretation can change entirely your intended message.

Many types of adjectives create confusion rather than clarity in writing, so take care to provide readers with the most accurate and specific terms possible. Generalizations about height and weight, quantity, and quality pose similar problems in interpretation.

> Being a *tall* man is not as much fun as some people think.

How tall is "a tall man"? Is the "tall man" pictured by a reader who is five feet six inches in height the same as the one pictured by a reader who is six feet? Is "tall" used to describe any man whose height exceeds the designated "average" height used by life insurance companies—or the "average" height used by the federal government in calculating health risks? (The two differ.) Provide a specific number as early in the writing as possible, so that you and the reader are thinking about the same information.

> The funeral for Reverend Cash was attended by *many* friends and relatives.

How many people actually did attend the funeral that the writer describes as attended by "many friends and relatives"? How many will a reader imagine? Is the imagined number the same for readers who consider thirty people to comprise a crowd as for readers who find having three hundred people present to be insufficient? Even if you cannot provide an exact number, you will increase your credibility with readers if you make the attempt to provide a reasonably accurate approximation.

> Most parents were shocked to be confronted by a math teacher who was *carelessly dressed* and *verbally abusive* toward them.

What is the reader's perception of how the math teacher looked? Does "carelessly dressed" mean that the teacher's clothing was simply too casual for the observer's taste? Was the clothing dirty and wrinkled? Were the various pieces of clothing worn by the math teacher mismatched? How serious a fashion crime did the teacher commit? What does "verbally abusive" mean to you? To your reader? Did the math teacher shout orders at the parents? Had the parents expected the math teacher to show more deference to them? Were parents confronted by a tirade of insults and cursing?

The writers of these sentences simply do not present their ideas effectively by using vague modifiers, because too much is left to the understanding and the imagination. More effective communication would result if the sentences were rewritten, as in the following examples:

> Standing *six feet seven inches* in my stocking feet is not as much fun as some people think.

The funeral for Reverend Cash was attended by nearly *three hundred* friends and relatives.

Most parents were shocked to be confronted by a math teacher who *wore dirty blue jeans and a tattered sweatshirt* and *who called them idiots.*

Strong, specific verbs reach out and grab the attention of readers, but too many writers become accustomed to using a small group of safe verbs from which they rarely deviate, leaving readers to only imagine the range of actions attached to the subject of the verb. Other writers fall into the "got" trap, substituting a form of "to get" in the place of many other verbs with more precise meanings, leaving readers unsure of just how much interest the writer has in the topic. Using vibrant verbs, those which provide specific meaning and identify specific actions, is one way a writer can excite the interest of readers while enriching their understanding of the topic.

Why settle for boring verbs when language is so rich with possibilities? Consider how much more interesting you can make the following sentences by substituting strong action verbs for the bland choices of the writer.

The mayor *walked* out of the council meeting after Dr. Angles *suggested* changes in the housing authority code.

Do the words in italics create a strong visual image? Did the mayor overreact when he walked out of a meeting after someone merely suggested changes? If this is correct, then retain the bland, boring verbs. Consider how much more interesting this sentence becomes if the writer substitutes specific action verbs for those in italics. Was the mayor angered? If so, then a more accurate description would be to write that the mayor "stormed," "stomped," "rushed," or "barreled" out of the meeting. The second verb is also far too vague to give readers a sense of what actions by Dr. Angles might have created the specific reaction by the mayor. To what did the mayor react? Might Dr. Angles have done more than merely suggested changes? Is it possible that he "demanded," "ordered," "required," or "advocated" changes?

Readers of the sentence above might view the situation with more seriousness if the writer attached more importance to identifying the actions of the two men. Would you be tempted to read further to learn more about the issue? Most readers would, because a revised sentence containing the more specific verbs indicates conflict, and conflict is always interesting.

Examine the following sentences and observe the effect that changing the verbs has on your level of interest as a reader, as well as the way in which meaning changes when the substitutions are made.

### Example 1

The caretaker *took* the gold statue and *placed* it in the closet.

### Example 2

The caretaker *stole* the gold statue and *hid* it in the closet.

### Example 3

The caretaker *removed* the gold statue and *stored* it in the closet.

### Example 4

The caretaker *confiscated* the gold statue and *safeguarded* it in the closet.

By changing one or both verbs, the writer can effectively alter the reader's perceptions of the caretaker and his actions regarding the gold statue. Is the caretaker simply carrying out an expected task, as examples 1 and 3 imply? Is the caretaker a thief, as example 2 suggests? Or has the caretaker recognized the statue as illegally obtained property and put it aside until the proper authorities can take possession of it? The choice of verbs makes the difference in the writer's message and the reader's understanding of the incident by adding more specific meaning to the action.

As mentioned above, in addition to using bland, boring, and vague verbs, many writers also inundate their work with the all-purpose verb "to get." Avoiding the "get syndrome" calls upon your skills in achieving both verb variety and precise diction. How can you avoid this pitfall? The most effective means of avoiding the "get syndrome" is to remain alert to overuse of this verb. Become adept at using more specific verbs to accurately say what you mean.

Review the use of "to get" in the following sentences. How can each be more effective? What verb can you substitute in each to make the action more specific?

### Example 1

How much money do you *get* each week as a teacher?

### Example 2

I don't *get* what you mean by that response.

### Example 3

The school district is hoping to *get* $3 million in federal funds.

### Example 4

The scholarship winner was able to *get* high grades throughout her high school career.

### Example 5

We were not able to *get* a quote from the mayor.

Do you overuse "get" in conversation? Most people do, and they carry such misuse over into their writing. Each of the five examples above conveys a message to readers, but they all resort to using the weak, nonexpressive verb "to get," instead of exploiting the potential of strong action verbs. Observe how much more expressive each question or statement becomes when a strong verb is substituted.

### Example 1

How much money do you *earn* each week as a teacher?

### Example 2

I don't *understand* what you mean by that response.

### Example 3

The school district is hoping to *receive* $3 million in federal funds.

### Example 4

The scholarship winner was able to *achieve* high grades through-out her high school career.

### Example 5

We were not able to *elicit* a quote from the mayor.

These examples contain only five of the many ways in which sentences containing the overused, all-purpose verb "to get" can become more effective by replacing "get" with verbs that express specific actions.

Writers can also achieve economy and effectiveness by eliminating the many **empty phrases** that function as "crutch phrases" for the inexperienced and unsure and replacing them with concise terms that make the point swiftly. When writing an essay, you should not feel the need to state, "in my opinion," "I feel," "I think that," "one must admit that," and similar phrases that appear intended to warn readers in advance that you desire less severe scrutiny of the ideas expressed because they are only based on your personal views. An essay is by definition a personal expression of opinion, unless otherwise stated, so the "crutch phrases" become redundant. The examples below contain only a few of the many unnecessary phrases that can be eliminated from writing or shortened significantly without detracting from the message. In most cases, using more concise phrasing increases the writing's effectiveness.

Our company was planning an affair *along the lines of* an awards dinner dance for the outgoing board of trustees.

*As a matter of fact,* the price per share of stock in the Audubon Corporation has risen steadily over the last year.

The city council is not open to a change of zoning laws *at the present time,* but they might consider a proposal during the next fiscal year.

The publication of his new book about the bombing of Hanoi will be delayed *because of the fact* that many Vietnam-era veterans contest the accuracy of the account.

*Due to the fact that* the second-semester grades have been completely obliterated by the computers, no one will be graduating from XYZ College this June.

This school district has contacted a consulting firm *for the purpose of* information about continuing education courses to meet the state requirements for public school teachers.

After being trained during six weeks at MCB Camp Lejeune, the troops will *have the ability to* infiltrate enemy territory and survive off the land.

The Federal Reserve Board lowered interest rates several times this year *in order to* slow the rate of inflation and to prevent a severe recession.

The Yankees failed to win a fourth World Series in 2001, *in spite of the fact* that they exerted a valiant effort.

*In the final analysis,* litigation may be the only recourse if a building contractor refuses to complete work within the contracted time.

The renovations of the high school stadium and the new fiberglass bleachers will cost *in the neighborhood of* $60,000.

The picketers plan to remain outside of the governor's mansion *until such time as* the governor meets with them and discusses their demands.

Each of the preceding sentences should be edited to eliminate the inflated phrasing and to sharpen the focus of the writing. Below are revised versions of the sentences in which the phrases italicized in the sentence examples have been reduced to one word. The revised sentences are shorter than the originals, and they are also more precise in expressing the writer's meaning.

Our company was planning an awards dinner dance for the outgoing board of trustees.

*In fact,* the price per share of stock in the Audubon Corporation has risen steadily over the last year.

The city council is not *currently* open to a change of zoning laws, but they might consider a proposal during the next fiscal year.

The publication of his new book about the bombing of Hanoi will be delayed *because* many Vietnam-era veterans contest the accuracy of the account.

*Because* the second-semester grades have been completely obliterated by the computers, no one will be graduating from XYZ College this June.

This school district has contacted a consulting firm *for* information about continuing education courses to meet the state requirements for public school teachers.

After being trained during six weeks at MCB Camp Lejeune, the troops will *be able to* infiltrate enemy territory and survive off the land.

The Federal Reserve Board lowered interest rates several times this year *to* slow the rate of inflation and to prevent a severe recession.

The Yankees failed to win a fourth World Series in 2001, *although* they exerted a valiant effort.

*Finally,* litigation may be the only recourse if a building contractor refuses to complete work within the contracted time.

The renovations of the high school stadium and the new fiberglass bleachers will cost *about* $60,000.

The picketers plan to remain outside of the governor's mansion *until* the governor meets with them and discusses their demands.

Precision in language is not only related to using the specific noun, adjective, adverb, or verb—it also requires that writers avoid the **jargon** that so many believe exhibits their knowledge. In its most limited meaning, jargon is the specialized language or terminology used by people who share a common occupation or activity. Actors use theater jargon, computer programmers use technical jargon, attorneys use legal jargon, police officers use law enforcement jargon, and many other professions and trades have their own terms that are familiar to individuals belonging to the profession or group. If you are writing for a specific group, you may expect to be understood if you use the jargon with which they will be familiar, but you cannot count on the same in a general reading audience.

Aside from jargon that consists of terms unique to a profession, some writers also use inflated language that does not relate directly to a profession, but is intended to impress readers and to create a distance between the writer and the reading audience. Such language is often labeled "officialese," because it appears mainly in reports, letters, and memoranda sent out by government agencies, large businesses, the military, and colleges and universities.

The following sentences contain common examples of such jargon.

Training seminars have been offered in the attempt to *ameliorate* the lack of prompt response time of the EMS units.

The board of trustees intends to *commence* fund-raising activities after the holiday season has passed.

The Department of Defense has purchased engine *components* from Antiquity Auto for its World War II–era jeeps.

Members of the base command will *endeavor* to provide adequate housing for the families of soldiers sent overseas.

Dr. Davis is a very busy researcher who never manages to *finalize* a project.

The drop in interest rates will positively *impact on* the number of low-income families who want to buy homes.

The board of education has decided that ten or more days' absence is a strong *indicator* that a teacher is not serious about working in this district.

For the *optimal* flavor, mix twice the amount of chocolate syrup in your milk.

The examination of textbooks used as a supplement to regularly assigned works goes beyond the *parameters* of our authority.

Before offering an opinion about what has been the most interesting period in economic history, *peruse* the following notes.

Stephen King was a high school English teacher *prior to* publishing the best-selling novel *Carrie.*

The writer who wants to establish the clearest communication with readers should *utilize* precise and specific language.

After meeting for several hours, the representatives of the individual branches of the armed forces reported that they had created a *viable* plan.

The general jargon in these sentences renders them hard to read and unfriendly to readers. The revised versions below convey the writer's message in plain English, making the writing more accessible. The words that have been substituted for the jargon appear in italics.

Training seminars have been offered in the attempt to *improve* the lack of prompt response time of the EMS units.

The board of trustees intends to *begin* fund-raising activities after the holiday season has passed.

The Department of Defense has purchased engine *parts* from Antiquity Auto for its World War II–era jeeps.

Members of the base command will *try* to provide adequate housing for the families of soldiers sent overseas.

Dr. Davis is a very busy researcher who never manages to *finish* a project.

The drop in interest rates will positively *affect* the number of low-income families who want to buy homes.

The board of education has decided that ten or more days absence is a strong *sign* that a teacher is not serious about working in this district.

For the *best* flavor, mix twice the amount of chocolate syrup in your milk.

The examination of textbooks used as a supplement to regularly assigned works goes beyond the *limits* of our authority.

Before offering an opinion about what has been the most interesting period in economic history, *look over* the following notes.

Stephen King was a high school English teacher *before* publishing the best-selling novel *Carrie*.

The writer who wants to establish the clearest communication with readers should *use* precise and specific language.

After meeting for several hours, the representatives of the individual branches of the armed forces reported that they had created a *workable* plan.

**Pretentious language** also clutters up writing. A writer may produce ornate and wordy language and sentences filled with large or obscure words to sound profound, but the result is often so confusing that the reader has no idea of the writer's message. An extensive vocabulary can be useful, but using archaic or obscure words in everyday writing is unnecessary. Judge a word by the value it adds to your attempts to communicate, not by the number of letters it contains. Consider the following sentence and decide how to edit it to make the meaning clearer.

> Each year, during the *annual* celebration of *our nation's independence on the fourth day in the seventh month of the year,* our town caters to the *vulgar inhabitants* and provides a *pyrotechnical* display.

The language of this sentence is pretentious and redundant, because "Each year" and "annual" state the same information. The writer may believe that the use of such terms as "our nation's independence," "vulgar [in its meaning of common or ordinary] inhabitants," and "pyrotechnical" show profound thinking, but readers will probably view them differently. There is no reason for the writer to laboriously identify "the fourth day in the seventh month of the year"—the date alone is sufficient. The revised sentence below is more understandable and friendlier.

> Each year during the July fourth celebration, the town provides residents with a fireworks display.

**Euphemisms** also detract from writing, although these phrases or words substituted for thoughts or terms that make some people uncomfortable, or which may considered harsh-sounding or ugly, may sometimes be appropriate. In formal writing, however, most euphemisms are needlessly evasive and often mislead readers because they obscure meaning. A euphemism may be appropriate when it is used to soften unpleasant experiences, as when we say that a pet has been "put to sleep." In your reading, however, you will find a broad range of euphemisms appearing in government reports, business profiles, news accounts, and other official writing. These create a psychological distance that also prevents the full importance of the writing from breaking through. The following sentences contain euphemisms commonly found in the writing of government, military, business, and higher education.

> In 1973, the United States Supreme Court determined that community standards would determine what was obscene and qualified as *adult entertainment.*

The renowned author checked into a prestigious health clinic to deal with his *chemical dependency.*

Most residents of suburbs protest strongly against government attempts to locate a *correctional facility* in their neighborhoods.

The large manufacturing plant announced plans to *downsize* employees in the coming fiscal year.

Many successful celebrities make a point of telling interviewers that, although currently wealthy, they were *economically deprived* as children.

The police spokesperson told the reporters at the press conference that experts identified an *incendiary device* as the source of the explosion.

Corporations that have not been particularly successful frequently report *negative growth* in several quarters of the year.

After the holiday bills arrive in the mail, many consumers will learn that they have greater *negative savings* than they imagined.

The upscale advertising agency changed the image of Joe's Car Lot by creating a campaign for the *pre-owned vehicles* the company sells.

The federal government has many uses for the *revenue enhancers* that are collected each year.

As the economy worsens many workers may find themselves *selected out* because of lessening profits.

Military officials reported that the three-day siege of the rebel stronghold ended in the *strategic withdrawal* of all ground troops.

Euphemisms often make a writer feel that readers will be more open to the message of the writing, but their misuse or overuse is just as likely to obscure the meaning. The following rewritten sentences, which eliminate the euphemisms, provide a more straightforward message.

In 1973, the United States Supreme Court determined that community standards would determine what was obscene and qualified as *pornography.*

The renowned author checked into a prestigious health clinic to deal with his *drug addiction*.

Most residents of suburbs protest strongly against government attempts to locate a *prison* in their neighborhoods.

The large manufacturing plant announced plans to *lay off* employees in the coming fiscal year.

Many successful celebrities make a point of telling interviewers that, although currently wealthy, they were *poor* as children.

The police spokesperson told the reporters at the press conference that experts identified a *bomb* as the source of the explosion.

Corporations that have not been particularly successful frequently report *losses* in several quarters of the year.

After the holiday bills arrive in the mail, many consumers will learn that they have greater *debts* than they imagined.

The upscale advertising agency changed the image of Joe's Car Lot by creating a campaign for the *used cars* the company sells.

The federal government has many uses for the *taxes* that are collected each year.

As the economy worsens many workers may find themselves *fired* because of lessening profits.

Military officials reported that the three-day siege of the rebel stronghold ended in the *retreat* of all ground troops.

---

**◻▭ QUICK TIP ▬▬◄**
# Keep It Simple

Use specific nouns, modifiers, and verbs in your writing to present a straightforward message. Avoid jargon, pretentious language, and euphemisms in favor of clear, honest language.

**SELF-TEST**

The writer of the following passage has included vague and imprecise language, jargon, pretentious words, and euphemisms. Edit to eliminate these, and rewrite the passage to express the content in precise diction and specific verbs.

At the present time, many companies located in the area have reported negative gains and are expected to announce plans to downsize some employees in the near future. Gopher and Sons Corporation will experience significant restructuring in the nature of other companies of similar size. Those who are down-sized will get a nominal amount of money when they leave, and a company spokesperson has told the media that in spite of the fact that finances are tight, the company believes at this point in time that none of the former employees and their families will be economically deprived. Due to the fact that reported earn-ings have been low in recent quarters, several top executives of the company have not gotten raises or bonuses in several years in spite of the fact that they have worked hard to make changes within the organization. Officials are taking steps to ameliorate the situation, but there are parameters of what they can do to produce a viable alternative to help those who have been se-lected out at this point in time. Because of the fact that the present plant facility is so old and the business has experienced negative growth in the past few years, owners have said that they will get money through loans to renovate and save jobs. The cost will be in the neighborhood of $8 million, and the work will be very ambitious. Everyone seems ready to do anything necessary to save the company, for the reason that the commu-nity depends on it. In the final analysis, recovery for the com-pany may have to wait until such time as the United States economy gets stronger.

Here is one example of how the passage could be rewritten more precisely:

Currently, thirty of the thirty-eight companies located in Alvers Township have reported losses and are expected to announce plans to lay off a total 1,000 employees at the end of July. Gopher and Sons Corporation will experience significant change like other companies of similar size. Those who are laid off will receive a one-time payment of $3,000 when they leave, and a company spokesperson has assured the media that, although finances are tight, the company believes now that none of the former employees and their families will be financially destitute. Because reported earnings have averaged one percent in the last seven quarters, the four top executives of the company have not gotten raises or bonuses in two years, though they have worked hard to make changes within the organization. The owner and chairman of the board of Gopher Corporation are seeking loans and selling off property to improve the situation, but there are limits to what they can do to produce a workable alternative to help those who have now been fired. Because the present plant facility is 120 years old and the business has experienced losses in the past few years, owners have said that they will obtain money through loans to renovate and save jobs. The cost will be about $8 million, and the work will include extensive renovations of existing buildings and new construction. The Alvers town council, local chamber of commerce, and even townspeople seem ready to do anything necessary to save the company, because the jobs of many members of the community and the businesses of its stores depend on it. Finally, recovery for the company may have to wait until the United States economy gets stronger.

# Selecting the Appropriate Voice

Writing that jumps off the page and engages readers immediately has a better chance of being read thoroughly and of conveying the writer's complete message than does writing that reaches its point in a roundabout manner. Readers respond to action, and your choice of verb should relate the actor directly and swiftly to the action rather than reveal the connection indirectly. **Passive-voice** verbs reverse the usual subject-verb-object sentence order and slow down a sentence because the subject is not performing the action of the verb and events or results are identified before their causes. Something is being done to the subject, but who or what is performing that action is often unclear. In contrast, **active-voice** verbs clearly tell the reader who is doing an action, and they move a sentence along at a swift pace. The following examples illustrate this difference.

> **Passive:** Shops *were closed* and windows *were barred* to protect store owners against the riot.
>
> **Passive:** Shops *were closed* and windows *were barred* by shop-keepers to protect themselves against the riot.
>
> **Active:** The store owners *closed* their shops and *barred* their windows to protect themselves against the riot.
>
> **Passive:** The research papers that students wrote two months earlier *were returned*.
>
> **Passive:** The research papers written two months earlier *were returned* to students.
>
> **Active:** The history professor *returned* the research papers that students wrote two months earlier.
>
> **Passive:** The prison *was stormed* by American troops, who found fourteen survivors.
>
> **Passive:** Fourteen survivors were found when the prison *was stormed* by American troops.
>
> **Active:** American troops *stormed* the prison and *found* fourteen survivors.

Read each trio of sentences aloud and listen carefully to the different effect that the active voice produces. You know immediately who the actors are and what they did. Reading the first passive choice, you learn that something was done to the subject, but not who performed the action. The second passive choice in each group slows you down even further by adding a phrase to identify the actor in each instance. The passive sentences lack vitality.

Are there situations when the passive voice is appropriate in your writing? Of course. Although you should use the active voice as frequently as possible, some writing situations make the passive voice mandatory.

Idiomatic expressions or common usage dictate the use of some passive verbs:

Police *were called* to the scene.

Their spirits *were dampened* by the rain.

Court *was adjourned* until nine o'clock Tuesday morning.

The dying man *was given* last rites.

The passive voice is also more appropriate in sentences that focus more on potential results than on who will achieve those results. In some cases, the subject may be truly unknown, yet the result is a key element in, if not the focus of, the story, so the passive voice is more appropriate.

In cases of civil disturbances, National Guard troops *are called* to quell an uprising.

Plans to build a new field house on campus *have been deferred* until the projected state budget has passed.

In our city, new council members *are elected* only if someone dies.

The passive voice is also useful as a means of distancing yourself from a writing, especially one that is based on a personal experience or when you have been part of the action or event related in the writing. Although many might argue that first-person narration should be used to convey experiences in which you have participated, good sense regarding the subject matter must dictate whether to use active voice with first-person narration or the passive voice to distance yourself. A writing intended as a mood piece or personal account will be more effective if you use the active voice, because this type of writing places the focus on the writer and not on the subject.

I *asked* the members of the crowd if anyone had seen the widow of the man we were honoring.

I *watched* with pride as bulldozers and people wielding sledge-hammers brought down the massive Berlin Wall.

To place the focus on the subject or topic, rather than on the individual providing the account, use the passive voice.

Members of the crowd *were asked* if anyone had seen the widow of the man we were honoring.

The massive Berlin Wall *was brought down* by bulldozers and people wielding sledgehammers.

Another instance in which the passive voice is used, and often extensively, is in the government reports or official statements of actions that politicians and government agencies have taken. Rarely does a specific committee or other unit of government take or assign responsibility for an action. Thus, writings of this sort are dominated by the passive voice, in the manner of the following:

The new policy governing campus parking *was decided* by a faculty-student senate.

The fate of the bill *was decided* in a closed caucus.

The antiabortion information *was handed* out by the agency.

By now, you may believe that the active and passive voices are divorced from each other, but they are not. Instances do exist in your writing in which both voices are needed to provide necessary variation in sound and in rhythm to avoid monotony. Even continuous brisk action can become boring and should be interrupted with the slowing effects of sentences written in the passive voice. Integrating passive verbs into a narrative breaks up the action and provides variety of expression. Examine the following passage, which contains only active-voice verbs, and assess how successfully the writer engages your interest as reader.

Yankee fans *arrive* at the stadium at 2 P.M. on the day before the box office opens to purchase season tickets for the following year. The cold morning air *makes* some of them shiver. Some *wear* heavy coats and mufflers, and they *pull* their coats tightly around their bodies. All *focus* their eyes on the ticket windows. They *carry* their money and credit cards in their pockets, ready for use.

Several people *pass* cigarettes to each other, and groups *huddle* together for warmth. Everyone *enjoys* the common experience. Security guards *keep* the crowd in line, but they *treat* the fans in a friendly manner. They are also fans and *enjoy* their own working association with the historic stadium.

Everyone *stares* forward, waiting for the time to move quickly and the ticket window to open. When 9 A.M. *comes* and the tickets finally *go* on sale, both fans and security guards *feel* relief. No violence *has occurred,* but the huge crowd *knows* that anything could have happened in that situation.

The passage contains only active verbs, making it move along fairly quickly, but the active voice also creates a somewhat terse tone. Because the subject matter is based on a personal account, the writer could choose first-person narration, but wisely does not: the use of "I" throughout would distract strongly from the power of the account. Nonetheless, a more relaxed tone is appropriate for the subject matter, and the writer can achieve that tone by using passive verbs at key points in the passage. Consider how the passage relaxes and becomes reader-friendly when some of the active verbs become passive.

Yankee fans arrive at the stadium at 2 P.M. on the day before the box office opens to purchase season tickets for the following year. The cold morning air makes some of them shiver. Some wear heavy coats and mufflers, which *are pulled* tightly around their bodies. Their eyes *are focused* on the ticket windows, and their money and credits *are kept* in their pockets, ready for use.

Cigarettes *are passed* around as groups huddle together for warmth. Everyone enjoys the common experience. The crowd *is kept* in line by security guards, who treat the fans in a friendly manner. They are also fans and enjoy their own working association with the historic stadium.

Everyone stares forward, waiting for the time to move quickly and the ticket window to open. When 9 A.M. comes

---

╾══╾ **QUICK TIP** ══▶

# Choose Active Voice

Make the actor and subject of the sentence the same. Active verbs are direct and move the writing forward. Passive verbs are weak and offer information in a roundabout way. Be direct.

---

and the tickets finally go on sale, relief *is felt* by both fans and security guards. No violence has occurred, but the huge crowd knows that anything could have happened in that situation.

The tone of the passage changes when the writer converts six of the eighteen active verbs to passive verbs to eliminate the repetitive sound and rhythm created by the use of only active verbs. By scattering the use of passive voice throughout the passage, the writer improves the flow of the language and alters the pace of the account.

**SELF-TEST**

The following passage contains good organization, adequately developed ideas, and appropriate grammar, but the writer's overuse of the passive voice weakens the writing. Rewrite the paragraph, reviewing each verb to identify the passive verbs, and decide whether changing from the passive voice to the active voice would benefit individual sentences and the writing as a whole.

Many "baby boomers" remember their college years with a special fondness, but those days may just be "the good old days" that never happened. In the 1960s, many male students were given the option of serving their country or working to earn good grades in college, while others were drafted by the government without being given a choice. Those who were accepted by colleges saw higher education as a means of escape from the Vietnam War. They were motivated to succeed in school by the threat of receiving a letter from Uncle Sam offering greetings and an invitation to report to an induction center.

Once on campus, some formerly apathetic young adults were recruited by militant and moderate student organizations to participate in the antiwar movement, while others were influenced by the same organizations to become increasingly pro-war. Although women students were also recruited by the antiwar organizations, pioneering efforts were being made by them to break into formerly male-dominated professions. Record numbers of applications to medical school, law school, and graduate business programs were sent by women. The expectation of homemaking as a woman's post-college occupation was set aside as young women explored new professions. The system was also tested by African Americans, and they were often obstructed by the established government in their efforts to gain full equality. The United States was bombarded by change, as both men and women were confronted with new choices and new challenges. The lives of the baby boomers were formed by those experiences. When the men and women in America who are now in middle to late middle age are made to feel nostalgic by images of the 1960s, they are reacting to what they are told by their memories to recall. They would be disappointed by the truth of what they really experienced.

_____

_____

_____

**ANSWER**

Here is one way of revising the passage. The passive verbs are italicized. Review the rewritten version and compare it with yours.

### Rewritten Version

Many "baby boomers" remember their college years with a special fondness, but those days may just be "the good old days" that never happened. In the 1960s, the federal government gave many male students the option of serving their country or working to earn good grades in college, while the government drafted others without giving them a choice. Those whom the colleges accepted saw higher education as a means of escape from the Vietnam War. The threat of receiving a letter from Uncle Sam offering greetings and an invitation to report to an induction center motivated them to succeed in school. Once on campus, some formerly apathetic young adults *were recruited* by militant and moderate student organizations to participate in the antiwar movement, while others *were influenced* by the same organizations to become increasingly pro-war. [*The passive nature of the students in being recruited is best conveyed through the use of the passive voice in this sentence.*] Although women students *were also recruited* by the antiwar organizations, they made pioneering efforts to break into formerly male-dominated professions. Women sent record numbers of applications to medical school, law school, and graduate business programs. Young women set aside the expectation of homemaking as a woman's post-college occupation to explore new professions. African Americans also tested the system, and the established government often obstructed them in their efforts to gain full equality. Change bombarded the United States, as new choices and challenges confronted both men and women. The lives of the baby boomers *were formed* by those experiences. [*The passive nature of the students in being recruited is best conveyed through the use of the passive voice in this sentence.*] When images of the 1960s make men and women in America who are now in middle to late middle age feel nostalgic, they are reacting to what their memories recall. The truth of what they really experienced would disappoint them.

# Avoiding Bias in Writing

Writing is a powerful tool that can change opinions, clarify or destroy understandings, establish or disrupt rapport, and make important positive or negative differences in the lives of readers. The language you use does all of this and more, so choose your words carefully. One thoughtless reference or carelessly used pronoun in your writing is sufficient to create negative perception and destroy common ground with your reader.

To establish a rapport with readers, try to avoid stereotypes and assumptions about gender, race, ethnicity, age, class, religion, geographi cal location, physical or mental ability, and sexual orientation. Before you include references to the practices or characteristics of a particular group, consider carefully whether such references are necessary for your readers to understand the message and whether they are unnecessary or actually offensive. Many references are unnecessary, as in the following sentences:

> The council includes a doctor, a minister, a *woman firefighter,* and a *Muslim attorney.*

> After the election, the mayor appointed three members to the city development committee: attorney Jaime Deane, accountant Dean James, and *Mrs.* Mary Maine, teacher and *the mother of three.*

> Among contestants in the essay contest were Jim Smith, an *elderly* village resident; Lois Lane, a *girl* reporter; Leila Rhine, a *paraplegic* who also paints; and village *blue blood* Iva Bundel.

The writer of the first example may have intended to provide readers with specific information or to point to the diversity of the council members, but the result is more offensive than informative. To identify the firefighter by gender and the attorney by religion suggests that the writer finds it unusual that a woman might be a firefighter and surprised that a person of Muslim faith could be an attorney, yet the writer does not specify "male doctor" and "male minister," or even identify the religious affiliation of the minister. If the point is to exhibit diversity, then the religion and gender of each member of the council should be identified, or all such references eliminated. Either way, be consistent.

In the second example, the writer has shown no interest in identifying the marital status nor the parenting status of the two new male committee members, but the female member of the committee is clearly identified as married (or formerly married) and the mother of three children. Although the writer might have had nothing more in mind than the desire to provide complete information about Mary Maine, the references may also have a sinister intention to imply that Maine already leads a busy life and that she may not be as dedicated to her committee duties as the other two members. Readers are left to interpret the writer's motives.

The third example uses a negative age-related term, "elderly," that is irrelevant to the description of Jim Smith, unless the writer intends to convey a sense of how surprised everyone should be that someone of Smith's age could compete in such competition. If that is the writer's intention, then the derogatory connotation of the term "elderly" should be replaced by an exact age for Smith, which would allow readers to decide whether or not to be surprised. Describing Lane as a "girl reporter" appears intended to disparage her and to downplay her professionalism while it focuses on her relative youth. The description of Rhine as "a paraplegic who also paints" may show her creativity by identifying that she paints, but identifying her as having a physical disability seems unnecessary. In describing the final contestant, the writer unnecessarily identifies Iva Bundel as a member of the highest social class of the village, and "blue blood" is a term that is likely to alienate rather than inform readers.

If your writing does include such references, review your choices carefully—or ask someone more knowledgeable in the specific characteristics of a group to read the work—to make certain that the language is not offensive and that the group labels and references are accurate. Do not be surprised if a reader questions your assumptions and finds that the language you use signals disapproval of a group. You may also learn that you have subconsciously allowed stock responses to a group to enter your writing. Stock responses are stereotypes that we develop based on the variety of experiences and impressions with which the mass media bombard us. Because we do not always experience these impressions firsthand, they can lead to bias, bigotry, and intolerance toward particular groups, as well as perpetuating misunderstandings and half-truths. Even when such damaging perceptions are not stated directly, they lurk below the surface and result in unnecessary mention of group affiliation which can disrupt the writer's connection with readers.

Gender stereotypes in writing receive the most attention because they have long-standing associations with grammar. When trade publishers first revised their stylebooks three decades ago to caution writers to avoid sexism in language by eliminating use of the generic pronoun "he" in referring to indefinite pronouns (anybody, anyone, anything, each, either, everybody, everyone, everything, neither, nobody, none, no one, somebody, someone, something) or to generic nouns, the thought was revolutionary. Today, using "he" to refer to the singular noun representing a member of a group, such as a lawyer, a student, a doctor, a computer technician, or other formerly male-dominated profession is unacceptable and sexist, because such use appears to assume that only men hold such positions. Even if the writer knows this to be false and does not intend to convey this impression, the use of the generic pronoun "he" creates the perception of sexism. The perception of sexism also results when writers use the pronoun "she" in referring to the singular nouns representing members of formerly female-dominated professions, such as nurse, teacher, and librarian.

Pronoun gender bias can be easily eliminated by revising sentences to use both pronouns ("he or she"), using plural forms of the noun and pronoun reference, or eliminating pronouns entirely. Below are examples of how you can avoid sexist pronoun references.

A *police officer* must place *his* life on the line for others every day.

A *police officer* must risk *his or her* life for others every day.

*Police officers* must risk *their* lives for others every day.

A police officer faces life-threatening risks for others every day.

To succeed in the competitive entertainment world, *a gossip columnist* must cultivate *her* sources carefully.

To succeed in the competitive entertainment world, *a gossip columnist* must carefully cultivate *his or her* sources.

To succeed in the competitive entertainment world, *gossip columnists* must carefully cultivate *their* sources.

To succeed in the competitive entertainment world, a gossip columnist must carefully cultivate sources.

As the preceding examples show, the three alternatives are not all equally comfortable in all situations. Using the dual pronoun reference "his or her" is awkward, although grammatically correct, and eliminating the pronoun is not possible in all sentences without major revisions. The writer has to allow the topic of the writing to determine which approach to use in revising sentences in order to eliminate bias.

Specific words and phrases that call attention unnecessarily to members of either sex, to specific racial, ethnic, age, socioeconomic, or religious groups, or to people with serious illness or physical challenges—or that ignore or stereotype them—must also be eliminated from your writing. The list below contains a selection of the biased terminology you should excise from your writing, and alternatives for the terms.

## Avoiding Biased Terminology

| Biased Terminology | Suggested Alternative |
| --- | --- |
| actress | actor |
| AIDS victim | someone who has AIDS |
| American Indian | Native American |
| anchorman/anchorwoman | anchor |
| black American | African American |
| chairman/chairwoman | chair, chairperson, head, moderator |
| clergyman | clergymember, minister, pastor |
| coed | student |
| congressman/congresswoman | member of Congress, representative |
| Eskimo | Inuit |
| fireman/firewoman | firefighter |
| foreman | supervisor |
| freshman | first-year student |
| her old man | her husband |
| the little woman | wife |
| mailman | letter carrier, mail carrier, postal worker |
| male nurse | nurse |
| male secretary | secretary |
| man, mankind | humans, human beings, humankind, humanity, the human race |
| manpower | workers, personnel |
| matronly | *exact age* |
| Oriental | East Asian |
| policeman/policewoman | police officer |
| salesman/saleswoman | salesperson, salesclerk, sales associate |
| steward/stewardess | flight attendant |
| teenybopper | *exact age* |
| weatherman | weather forecaster, meteorologist |
| well-preserved | *exact age* |
| wheelchair-bound | uses a wheelchair |
| woman doctor | doctor |
| woman engineer | engineer |

---

┏━━┓ QUICK TIP ■━━━▶

# Consider the Feelings of Your Readers

Avoid words that carry stereotypes and assumptions about groups. Instead, use language that considers carefully the sensitivities of others and aids you in creating a common ground with readers.

---

**SELF-TEST**

The following passage contains words and phrases that express stereotypes and provide unnecessary identifications of group affiliation. Identify the biased terminology and write a revised, bias-free version.

Settling the American West was a difficult task that required supreme effort and often the supreme sacrifice of the frontier settlers. The Indians were savage beasts, and winters were harsh, especially if shelters had not been built by the time of the first snowfall. A settler could not depend upon nearby medical help and, if he became ill during the frigid winters, he would have only a small chance of surviving to spring. The fierce and hostile natural surroundings were only a part of his problem. Bloodthirsty Indians might attack at any time, without concern for the Christian lives they might obliterate. Even death would bring little solace, for few clergymen were available to provide the dead with a proper Christian burial. Fortunately, most settlers were uneducated and belonged to the lower economic classes. They had left their homes to find a better life in the West, so they were used to hardship and not as sensitive to suffering as their better-educated and more well-off contemporaries would have been.

_____

_____

_____

**ANSWER**

How does your rewrite compare to this revision?

### Revised Version

Establishing homesteads in the American West was a difficult task that required supreme effort and often the supreme sacrifice of the frontier settlers. The omnipresence of the Native Americans posed a constant threat, and winters were harsh, especially if shelters had not been built by the time of the first snowfall. Settlers could not depend upon nearby medical help, and those who became ill during the frigid winters would have only a small chance of surviving to spring. The fierce and hostile natural surroundings were only a part of the settlers' problem. Native American tribes who resented the intrusion on their lands might attack at any time and would fight fiercely for what belonged to them, often resulting in large numbers of deaths among the settlers. Even death would bring little solace for settlers, for few members of the clergy were available to provide the dead with a religious burial. Many of the settlers had experienced difficult lives that led them to leave their homes in the hope of finding better fortunes in the West. Because of their drive and determination, such settlers were willing to endure greater suffering than their better-educated and more well-off contemporaries, who headed West merely for sport.

---

## Make Your Prose Reader-Friendly

1. Use accurate and specific terms.
2. Avoid the temptation to dazzle readers with pretentious language and jargon.
3. Engage readers with active verbs.
4. Avoid bias-laden language and stereotyping.

Read carefully the following passage, taken from an assigned student essay on the topic of censorship of the Internet. Identify places in the passage where the writer uses vague or inaccurate terms, jargon, pretentious language, euphemisms, inappropriate voice, and biased terminology. Rewrite the passage to eliminate these errors.

The Internet belongs to everyone, although claims do continue to be heard that the Internet was invented by former vice president Al Gore. Some people today are trying to establish a claim of eminent domain. In my opinion, in spite of the fact that they have not been given any jurisdiction in the matter by authorities, they want to prevent the masses from enjoying free access to all areas of the Web. As individuals, we must extend the parameters of our authority and take it upon ourselves to ameliorate the situation or we will not get the freedoms that we deserve. If we are made to capitulate by these would-be censors, we may as well be in a correctional facility. As much as politicians, educators, and computer salespeople deny it, cruising the Internet is more an activity of younger people than of silver-haired old codgers or Christian moralists. Yet the cries for censorship of the Internet are pouring forth from the sector that least uses the entity—the senior citizens and the fundamentalists. Any computer-literate individual will tell you that he finds nothing offensive in being able to access information from the Internet on every topic imaginable. He would probably also provide examples of the many ways in which he and others have actually benefited from the available information. Data is given for free by organizations to people. News is provided online to Internet users by newspapers and television giants. Entertainment is made available to all ages by huge movie and music studios. The Internet is used widely by disabled people, AIDS victims, wheelchair-bound people, nerds, teenyboppers, and even Eskimos. This abuse must be fought by us, and the power of our lawmakers must be used by us. We must write letters to our congressmen, give petitions to our assemblymen, and lobby against such censorship by writing letters to our state senators and their wives. Such abuses of our freedom cannot be endured.

**ANSWER**

Compare your rewritten version to the version that follows, but remember that your changes might differ from those of the writer.

### Revised Version

The Internet belongs to everyone, although claims do continue that former vice president Al Gore invented it, and members of ultraconservative groups are trying to establish their own claims. Although the authorities have not given them any jurisdiction in the matter, they want to prevent others from enjoying free access to all areas of the Web. As individuals, we must extend our authority and work to correct the situation or we will not keep the freedoms that we deserve. If these would-be censors make us give in, we may as well be in prison. As much as politicians, educators, and computer salespeople deny it, cruising the Internet is more an activity of younger people than of older adults or religious reformers. Yet the sectors that least use the entity—older adults and religious reformers—have been the most vocal. All computer-literate individuals will tell you that they find nothing offensive in being able to access information from the Internet on every topic imaginable. They would probably also provide examples of the many ways in which everyone has actually benefited from the available information. Organizations provide free data to people. Newspapers and television giants provide news online to Internet users. Huge movie and music studios make entertainment available to all ages. Many other groups also make wide use of the Internet: people with physical and psychological disabilities, those who have AIDS, people who use wheelchairs, high-achieving students, teenagers, and even people who live in isolated northern areas, such as the Inuit. We must fight this abuse, and we must use the power of our lawmakers. We must write letters to our representatives in Congress, give petitions to our assembly officials, and lobby against such censorship by writing letters to our state senators and their spouses. Such abuses of our freedom cannot be endured.

# 9 Applying Your Skills to Academic Writing

## Objectives

In this chapter, you will learn to:

- respond to informational or essay test questions

- write an argumentative or persuasive essay

- develop a research essay

- report laboratory or scientific results

Academic writing requires the same strong writing skills and attention to detail as other types, but the nature of the writing may differ significantly. Many of the examples that appear in earlier chapters were taken from writings completed for academic assignments, but the concern in earlier chapters was on the organization, development, and language of the passages. The focus in this chapter is on structuring the writing to fulfill specific academic requirements and selecting content for greatest effectiveness.

# Writing the Informational
# or Test Essay Question

Unlike the stand-alone essay that students are asked to write in college composition classes, in which the topic may be personal and chosen by the student, the test essay question is highly regulated and must provide information known in advance by the professor. Students answering the question hope that they know the information and can correctly formulate their responses. Though the content of the thesis or topic sentence is typically taken out of the writer's hands, the organization and development of the material are still fully under the student's control.

Consider the paragraph you corrected earlier to eliminate stereotypes regarding Native Americans. It is also an essay response to the question: "What challenges did frontier settlers of the American West face in establishing homesteads?"

Establishing homesteads in the American West was a difficult task that required supreme effort and often the supreme sacrifice of the frontier settlers. Settlers faced dangers from both the environment and from the existing inhabitants of the frontier land. Winters were harsh, especially if shelters had not been built by the time of the first snowfall. Isolated as they were, settlers could not depend upon nearby medical help, and those who became ill during the frigid winters would have only a small chance of surviving to spring. The fierce and hostile natural surroundings were only a part of the settlers' problem. The omnipresence of the hostile Native Americans who resented their land being taken posed a constant threat, and they might attack at any time. They fought fiercely for what belonged to them, often causing large numbers of deaths among the settlers. The settlers' homes were attacked and often burned down in the middle of the night. Even with such hardship, the settlers persevered, because many had experienced difficult lives that led them to leave their homes in the hope of finding better fortunes in the West.

In responding to the question, the student rewords the essay question to provide a strong and focused opening statement. Doing so serves several purposes. The reader/grader sees that many of the key words of the question appear in the opening to the response, and this suggests that the

---

⌑ **QUICK TIP** ▬▬

## Essay Responses

Read all essay questions through several times, then write an introduction statement that rewords the question.

---

student has a firm grasp of the topic, even if this ultimately proves false. Rewording the question to provide an opening statement to the response is also helpful to the student, as it provides the student with structure and highlights important ideas with which the response must deal.

The second sentence of the response provides a generalized statement of the two specific points that will be developed in the body of the passage: support point #1, the threats posed by the harsh environment; and support point #2, the threats posed by the indigenous people. The writer then develops each threat separately with examples. To move smoothly from the development of one support point to the next, the writer includes a transition sentence that segues into the second support point. The concluding sentence of the passage sums up the discussion by referring to the opening sentence, and it also offers a brief explanation of why the settlers persevered.

# Writing the Argumentative Essay

Much of academic writing consists of taking a position or a stand, then supporting that point of view in a logical manner that shows the reader the validity of your position. Argumentative writing is an attempt to convince readers to agree with your point of view, to follow a course of action, or to make a specific decision you advocate. The support used in written argument depends strongly on well-chosen evidence and carefully controlled language that require more skill and organizational ability of the writer than other forms of writing. In developing an argument, the writer must predict readers' objections and provide evidence and discussion to offset those objections. The writer must also be careful to choose a writing strategy, language, and style that are most suitable to the subject and that will be most effective in convincing readers of the validity of the position. Perhaps most difficult of all, the writer cannot merely support a position. The most effective argumentative writing also acknowledges that other views on the subject exist, even as the writer convinces readers that the position taken is superior to all others.

Argumentative writing may be either logical or persuasive, and most argumentative essays contain elements of both approaches. The topic determines which type of appeal the writer will make.

The writer uses a **logical appeal** when the writing is not intended to make readers take a specific action. This approach appeals to readers' knowledge and understanding, often using proof and counterproof to develop the argument in a carefully reasoned movement that resembles a flowchart:

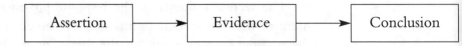

Logical argument avoids the use of emotional appeal, and most such writing will deal with legal issues, business or technical proposals, scientific or philosophical materials, or other writing that uses factual evidence. The writer may use either inductive or deductive reasoning as a pattern to present the support ideas. **Inductive reasoning** derives a general statement or conclusion from a group of specific examples. For example, a writer might examine the number of housing violations cases, driving violations, and theft charges that appear in day and evening court dates and conclude that the judge schedules the majority of one type of violation more often to be heard in the evening than in the day session. In contrast, **deductive reasoning** begins with a general statement to reach a specific conclusion. This type of reasoning is easily represented with a three-part argument, called a **syllogism,** which contains a **major premise,** a **minor premise,** and a **conclusion.**

**Major premise** All teachers in this state must prove themselves competent in the subject matter before being licensed to teach in a public school.

**Minor premise** Ms. Kalem is a licensed mathematics teacher in the local public school.

**Conclusion** Ms. Kalem has proven herself competent in mathematics.

These two patterns of reasoning are helpful in brainstorming and organizing ideas, but they are not foolproof. When using inductive reasoning, the writer might use too limited a set of specific examples, which may result in an incorrect generalization. Problems may also occur in deductive reasoning, especially if the major premise is inaccurate or patently false. As with all writing aids, use these patterns with caution and apply your own common sense in determining what is logical.

Persuasive writing, such as editorials, advertising, speechmaking, propaganda, and personal appeals, is more concerned with stirring others to take action than with building a logical argument. Writers of persuasive material use figurative language, varied speech rhythms, diction, slanted and biased prose, and tone to motivate the desired response. The following example could be made into a persuasive writing if the reader were to direct the discussion toward readers' emotions and their biases and prejudices. Instead, the writer has chosen to present evidence to support an argument that competency testing does not deliver what it promises.

### Periodic Competency Examinations for Teachers

National concerns about public education have led state education commissions to consider various means of assuring the competence of their teachers. Plans have ranged from relicensing and continuing education plans to various degrees of testing, all with the aim of keeping teachers strong in their major areas and competent in the classroom. Our state assembly has voted to require competency of teachers, but the effort does not offer much promise of success, as other states with the same requirement have reported.

One of the least expected disadvantages to required competency testing of teachers has been the manner in which it disrupts school life. Testing days are too numerous and require too much out-of-school time. Teachers become too preoccupied with studying and the quality of their work as well as the quality of their interaction with students and colleagues lessens. Some schools even report that the new constraints on the time of teachers lead many to deny students after-school help.

Despite the stated intention of increasing the quality of public education, competency testing of teachers comes at great cost to taxpayers. The states that require such testing have also demanded that school districts accommodate teachers who are to undergo competency testing at a given time. In some cases, the result is lost classroom time. A further cost of salaried time spent in preparation and test taking must be acknowledged, and individual school districts must also shoulder the costs of state-provided test-taking materials and state-contracted grading of the tests.

The professional results of required competency testing have not been as positive as early proponents once believed. Few studies of testing effectiveness have been conducted, but those states that have studied the results report that no significant differences in classroom benefit seem to result from the rigorous and time-consuming process. Some may argue that the benefits may take several years to emerge, but long-term results are hard to judge. What is definite from these studies is that the testing process has a negative effect on the lives of teachers and their families. Test preparation causes disruptions to teachers' lives, and mandatory test reviews are often held at inconvenient times. In many cases, teachers are required to spend large amounts of time studying in areas of the major they have not been teaching for years and will never teach, as long as they remain in the specific school district. Results also show that family life suffers as teachers are placed under increased pressure.

The planned requirement that teachers undergo periodic competency testing is a case of good intentions carried out in an ineffectual manner. Rather than raise classroom standards and increase learning in the public schools, such testing as it is now planned is more likely to further tarnish the image of teachers, because of the inevitable few failures and the emphasis in the media on their anxiety. This is a high price to pay if the results reported by other states show no appreciable benefit.

The preceding passage incorporates all of the guidelines for good writing that appear in the first eight chapters of this book, resulting in a well-organized, carefully developed discussion that contains a clear thesis, linked topic sentences, and specific support details. Based on a synthesis of evidence drawn from studies made in other states, the writer ends the argumentative passage with a clear, strong statement that argues against state competency testing of teachers.

In contrast to the care taken by the writer of the preceding passage to use fact and evidence to show that the position is correct, the next example of persuasive writing seeks to convince readers to boycott large manufacturers who do not produce quality products for consumers. The writer appeals to the emotions and uses a range of slanted language and figurative language (in italics) to achieve that end.

> Buy a new piece of electronic equipment today, and you can expect to *waste* your money, for it will last no longer than the warranty. Service contracts are time-limited, and many companies will only permit a consumer to purchase or renew contracts for up to five years after the purchase of certain equipment. Advertising *bombards unsuspecting* consumers with directives to buy new versions of old objects, even if the changes or improvements are *trivial* and only in regard to color or size, not in function. We must stop allowing the large manufacturers to *abuse hardworking* consumers, and we must take a stand against this *disposable* economy by boycotting the companies whose products have only a *short life span.*
>
> Most families have telephones, but few have owned the same telephone for more than a few years because the equipment manufactured over the last three decades is far less durable than the old black telephones made by Bell that once occupied most homes. Families of the 1950s and 1960s could *count on* their telephones to work through numerous falls off the table and after the receiver was *banged down* in anger many times. Those telephones were *survivors.* Today's telephones are *fragile* in comparison and should come with labels that warn consumers, "Handle with Care." *Sadly,* this *lack of quality* extends to numerous other products.
>
> Working radios and television sets from the first half of the twentieth century have become *prized* classic collectibles, but the same will not be said of the compact disc players and videocassette recorders of today. Even if care is taken to insert discs or videotapes, something usually goes wrong with the playing equipment within months of purchase. If you manage to keep yours working longer, you might find that you will *patronized* if you call an authorized service center several years later. Representatives will probably be *surprised* if your appliance has worked beyond five years. This unfortunate situation is not limited to small appliances, and even *big-ticket* items are now "disposable."

Classic car parades of the future will probably have to contain the same cars that are today considered classics, because the functioning lives of today's new models are limited. You may look with *awe* upon a *vintage* 1921 Model T, but be unable to find a car made in the 1970s or beyond, because most are sent to *rust* in *junkyards* after a decade or less. Part of the problem is our greedy society that demands more powerful and more prestigious transportation each year, but manufacturers are also to blame because they are not making cars that will last for decades.

We have become accustomed to items that break soon after purchase and service contracts that promise only a few years of product functioning. As a result, we actually feel *grateful* to own an item that gives *decent value* and has a reasonably *useful life span,* which we mistakenly view as our *privilege* rather than as our right as consumers. We should not continue to accept such *abuse.* Manufacturers who continue to sell *poorly made* products should be boycotted, and legislation must be passed to guarantee that consumers do not continue to be *victims* of planned obsolescence. Consumers must raise their expectations and prove to industry that we are not a disposable society.

The writers of both the logical argument and the persuasive passage have followed the same steps in organizing their ideas and developing their sequence of thought as must writers of any type of material. Their responsibility to readers is greater, however, because they must also take greater care to avoid faulty reasoning, also labeled *logical fallacies.* Among such fallacies are the following: *oversimplification* of solutions or ideas, *either/or thinking* that allows no other alternatives to those of the writer, *non sequiturs* in which the evidence does not logically relate to the writer's inferences or conclusions, *hasty generalizations* based on too little evidence,

---

**◁▭▭ QUICK TIP ▬▬▶**

## Arguing and Persuading

Use evidence and fact to develop an argumentative writing, but appeal to the emotions and use slanted language in persuasive writing.

*false analogies* that force connections between unconnected ideas, and *begging the question* by assuming that what is to be proven is already true.

# Developing the Research Essay

Writing a research essay requires a series of steps: generating a topic, researching the material, outlining the ideas, determining organization, documenting different types of sources, and presenting the material. These topics cannot be covered in this chapter, but they are handled in depth in easily available research handbooks. For the research essay, you are expected to have a familiarity with data-gathering and research techniques, and our focus is on identifying the ways in which your practice to this point is helpful in producing a well-written piece.

The research essay must contain the same required elements as all other essays: a strong introduction with a clear thesis statement; support paragraphs with topic sentences that relate directly to the thesis statement, and which are supported by specific details; and a concluding paragraph that summarizes or makes recommendations for further examination of the topic. The difference is that the research essay must be developed and supported by the documented ideas of others, and the references must be integrated with your text so that the reader is always aware of the source of any material taken from others.

A research essay must synthesize information taken from diverse sources, not merely summarize information derived from only one, as in the passage below:

> The existence of U.S. troops serving in Vietnam began in December 1961, with the arrival in Saigon of 400 uniformed army personnel, who were there to operate helicopter companies and not to serve as combat troops. By December 1962, the U.S. government had placed 11,200 military personnel in the country. The number grew to 27,000 in March 1965, when a brigade of U.S. Marines was positioned south of the demilitarized zone at Danang, and U.S. combat strength increased to 200,000 by December of that year. As U.S. leaders made attempts to end the war, troop buildups continued. In 1969, U.S. military strength in South Vietnam peaked at 541,000. (Source: *Funk & Wagnall's New Encyclopedia,* 1996)

A variety of materials must be found to support the assumptions of the writer of a research essay, and the sources must appear at appropriate points in the essay and include the last name of the author of the source work and the page numbers. Not all statistics need to be documented, nor do all opinions need to receive a citation in the following example, because some of the information may be considered general knowledge. The final page of the research essay should contain the complete identification information for all sources cited in the text. How you document your information and the structure of your citations will depend upon the style guide assigned or required: *Modern Language Association* (MLA), *Chicago Manual of Style, American Psychological Association* (APA), and others.

The events of September 11, 2001, have led many citizens of the United States to seek information about Afghanistan, a nation that formerly held little interest for them. Americans have consulted atlases and searched for information online, but many have been disappointed in what they have found. Afghanistan is not, in general, very interesting to the creators of travel and information guides; yet it is a land rich in culture and history, waiting to be discovered.

One of the world's least developed countries, Afghanistan is a seemingly nondescript nation located in southwestern Asia, but it has great potential for economic growth under proper management. Kabul is the capital city, also its largest. Rather sparsely populated, the nation has a population density of only 99 people per square mile. Afghanistan comprises 251,773 square miles, and the greatest distance from east to west in the country is 820 miles and from north to south 630 miles. It is a country of great topological contrasts, containing great mountains, scorching deserts, fertile valleys, and rolling plains (Jameson 2–13). The highest mountain is Nowshak, rising 24,557 feet above sea level, and the lowest point in the country is Sistan Basin, 1,640 feet above sea level. As diplomats have pointed out, Afghanistan lives in an uneasy state in times of peace, because it is bordered by Turkmenistan, Uzbekistan, and Tajikistan on the north, China on the far northeast, Pakistan on the east and south, and Iran on the west (Brzezinski 25). Although Afghanistan has about 11,700 miles of roads, it has no railroads. Moreover, most paved roads

---

◁▭▭▭▶ QUICK TIP ▬▬▬▷

# The Research Essay

Write a framework of your opinions, then insert material from others to support your opinions. Always include appropriate credit for the ideas of others.

---

were heavily damaged and made unusable in the 1980s during the war with the Soviet Union (*NYT,* October 12, 2001).

Many people have expected that significant change would occur in Afghanistan, because the population has nearly doubled in the last two decades, from 13,051,358 in 1979 to an estimated population of 24,977,000 for 2002 (*CIA Sourcebook*). Eighty percent of the residents live in rural areas, and most of the people fifteen years of age or older cannot read and write. Although the law requires all children from seven to fifteen years old to go to school, many of these children cannot. The country does not have enough schools or teachers, due largely to the upheaval caused by the past two decades of war (Kardan). In place of formal schooling, folklore, folk songs, and folk dances play an important part in Afghan life and enable the people to pass their values and traditions on from one generation to the next.

# Writing Laboratory or Scientific Results

The high school or college lab report often creates apprehension among students, who may feel intimidated by the language of scientific experimentation.

Each science department and even each instructor may have slightly different requirements for the laboratory reports students submit, but all are close in content to a standard format: abstract, introduction, methods and materials, results, description and conclusions, and references.

The **abstract** should be written after the entire work is completed, because it is a summary of the research approach, the results, and the conclusions. Avoid the temptation to write a too-detailed abstract, because

---

```
╔══════════════════════════════════════════════════╗
║              ▭▭▭ QUICK TIP ▬▬▶                    ║
║                                                    ║
║              The Laboratory Report                 ║
║                                                    ║
║  Use the standard format in presenting the results of scientific exper-  ║
║  iments. Be meticulous in reporting your data and explaining your         ║
║  procedures.                                                              ║
╚══════════════════════════════════════════════════╝
```

readers will have access to your findings later in the report. A recommended length for the abstract is no more than two hundred words.

The **introduction** explains the purpose of the experiment and provides a brief review of literature describing other studies on the topic. The studies examined should be relevant to the current research and offer readers synopses of the methods and findings.

In the **methods and materials** section, the writer should describe the experiment. Explain what approach was taken, and identify the materials that were used in conducting the experiment. In this section, also inform the reader of methods that were attempted but discarded.

The **results** section identifies methodically what the experiment produced at every stage of the effort. Each component and subject of the experiment should be addressed.

The **discussion and conclusions** section of the report is the lengthiest. In this section, the reader learns of the significance of the findings of the experiment. Based on the statistical analysis, the writer provides the conclusions of the experiment and either accepts or rejects the hypothesis.

The final section contains references for the studies reviewed in the introduction, as well as complete documentation for any other materials that the writer uses in the report.

# <u>10</u> Writing for Business

## Objectives

In this chapter, you will learn to:

- organize ideas for business memoranda and letters
- express ideas clearly in reports
- maintain clear communication in cyberspace

Business correspondence and reports communicate with readers in a specific, targeted manner, unlike most types of writing discussed to this point. Organization and development are still important, but ideas must be clear and concise, and the language must create and maintain good-will with readers as well as be polite and easily understood. In earlier discussions of writing, this book has emphasized the art of communicating with an audience and the need to determine who will read the work, but many writers recognize that only a bare approximation of the audience is possible in the types of writing discussed to this point. This is not so in business writing, because memoranda, letters, and reports are written for specific purposes and directed to specific individuals. For this reason, business writing is custom-created, and the writer has an even greater responsibility to write for maximum readability.

# Organizing Ideas for Business Memoranda and Letters

**Memoranda** are written and sent within an organization, letters are written to individuals or groups outside of an organization, and reports, which detail the results of studies and other data, may be directed either inside or outside the organization. What the three have in common is that they all require writing that is clear, concise, correct, consistent, and complete.

Because a memorandum is a form of written communication that is sent within a company, it contains no salutation ("Dear Mr. Jones") or complimentary close ("Sincerely"). All memoranda, however, should contain the following essential information: the date, the name of the person (or people) to whom the memorandum is addressed, the name of the person (or people) who sent the memorandum, the subject, and the body. Although most companies have their own formats for memoranda, the following model reflects the basic content:

Date:    November 20, 2001
To:      James Jones, Marketing Manager
From:    Ann Smith, Purchasing Manager
Subject: Surplus of purple artificial evergreen trees

We recently made a purchase of 20,000 purple artificial evergreen trees at a rate highly advantageous to this company, but to avoid having to warehouse them we would like to market them vigorously for the upcoming holiday season.

The trees can provide a substantial fourth-quarter profit for the company, so we are planning to do as quick a turnover as possible of the stock. To do this, our respective departments will have to act closely and quickly in the coming weeks.

Plan to meet at 10 A.M. on Friday, November 23, 2001, in our department office to work up a campaign strategy. With this heads-up on the situation, I hope to give you time to come up with a few workable marketing ideas to present at the meeting.

This example follows all of the guides for writing an effective memo. The text begins with a summary paragraph that contains the most important information, and moves to the directive in the final paragraph.

The writer is clear regarding the purpose of the memorandum and states without equivocation the reason for the proposed meeting and what will be expected of the marketing department at the meeting. Each paragraph focuses on only one idea, and the overall memorandum makes clear exactly what the writer wants the readers to do and when.

The standard **business letter** is very similar in content and intention to the memorandum, but it is sent outside of a company and requires a salutation and a closing. In addition, a letter usually contains a more friendly tone because the writer often attempts to persuade and cultivate readers' goodwill. Every letter should begin with a polite greeting, even if the subject of the letter is less than friendly. To be effective, the writer must show restraint and explain the purpose of the letter clearly and specifically in the first paragraph, including all details necessary for the reader to understand the issue. Once the intention of the letter is explained, the writer should provide the reader with a clear idea of what action, if any, the writer expects to be taken. The letter then closes on a positive note, with the writer's expression of appreciation for the reader's attention and a statement to motivate a response, which may supply the reader with the best times to reach the writer and the telephone or fax numbers or e-mail address to use.

The following sample letter uses only one of many formats that may be used in writing business letters; each company has its preferences.

**Boulabou Corporation**
*8321 Freedom Way*
*Bergmont, New Jersey 070XX*
*(555) 555-5555*

November 27, 2001

Mr. Smith Jones
Holiday Trees International
453 Noshow Road
Acheson, New Jersey 076XX

Dear Mr. Jones:
Boulabou Corporation has recently made a special purchase of 20,000 novelty purple artificial trees which our marketing department predicts will set a trend this holiday season. Before

we make an offer of these trees at a special price available to all of our clients, we are contacting those with whom we have worked most closely in the past. You can purchase these trees at only $5 per unit, with a 10% discount for 2,000 units or more.

To take advantage of this special offer, please contact me at extension 4322 or send me an e-mail at asmith@boulaboucorp.com. Place your order before our stock is depleted.

Cordially,

Ann Smith,
Purchasing Manager

## Expressing Ideas Clearly in Reports

Business **reports** are usually written as permanent documents that record any number of events and situations: a trip, a conference, a program, or the results of a study. Unlike the specific audiences of memoranda and letters, reports may be addressed internally to an individual, a department, or the parent company, or they may be created for individuals outside of a company or for an outside agency. In addition to providing permanent records of events, reports may also provide information that aids decision makers.

The size and formats for reports vary widely, from one paragraph for brief daily or weekly reports, to extensive volumes that provide information about long-term, major projects. Whatever their length, all reports require that writers include the following specific information for readers in the opening pages: date, list of recipients, originators, subject. The way a writer organizes the above information should follow company policy, but business reports usually contain the following format:

| | |
|---|---|
| Title page | Body |
| List of contents | Conclusions |
| List of illustrations and tables | Recommendations |
| Abstract | Appendices |
| Introduction | |

---

◁▭▭▷ QUICK TIP ▬▬▶

# Write to Be Understood

Use clear and concise language whether you are sending a memo to reprimand or a letter to establish goodwill. Make your intentions clear.

---

In completing the abstract, introduction, body, conclusions, and recommendations sections, the writer must use all of the techniques for clear writing discussed throughout this book.

The **abstract** should contain brief descriptions of the problem, the course of action taken in the study, the results achieved, the conclusions of the writer based on the results, and recommendations for further study.

The **introduction** should be jargon-free and accessible to general readers, while it provides background for the study described in the body of the report. The writer should include in the introduction an identification of the problem, the reason the study was conducted, the extent of the work, the methods used in conducting the study, and a general background to the topic or need for the study.

The **body** is the lengthiest part of a business report, because it provides details regarding the subject, as well as a complete discussion of earlier attempts to explore the subject, the specific approach used in the study, the specific actions taken to analyze the problem, the results of the study, and what the results prove.

The **conclusions** section is brief but very important to the report, because the writer must interpret the impact of the results on the company and on the broader community.

In the **recommendations** section, the writer must apply judgment to the results and provide suggestions regarding the implications of the results. The writer may recommend that further study be undertaken, that a specific purchasing decision be made, that the project be continued, or that other approaches be considered. Many readers will be most interested in the conclusions and the recommendations sections, because they provide implications for future actions.

The writer should place in the **appendices** the charts, tables,

---

```
━━━━━▭ QUICK TIP ◀━━━━
```

## Report—Don't Rehash

In your reports, provide readers with the information and analysis they need to make important decisions. Do not just summarize the procedures of a study or of related events.

---

documents, and other material that would disrupt the narrative of the report if integrated into the text. Each different type of material should be given its own appendix and designated by a letter of its own (Appendix A, Appendix B, Appendix C, and so on).

# Maintaining Clear Communication in Cyberspace

Electronic communication requires the same attention to clear writing as all other forms of written communication. Sending a hastily completed first draft of a memo, letter, report, or other writing via electronic means will have the same disastrous effects on your credibility and reputation as using the older methods of communication—and the result will be just as permanent. The reader can store your carelessly created writing in a computer file or print it out immediately, then study it closely at leisure, perhaps much to your chagrin.

As a general rule, treat all e-mail in the same way that you treat hard-copy writing. Clear writing is necessary in both, but the "smiley faces," lowercase letters, and abbreviated words that may be acceptable in personal e-mail sent between friends should never appear in formal communications such as letters, memoranda, reports, academic submissions, and the like. Such casual devices are not uncommon; many online college course instructors, including this author, have received numerous student assignments via e-mail that contain what we label "e-mail illiteracy." Students usually only submit assignments in that condition once, because online instructors in most disciplines will return the assignments ungraded and with the warning to formalize the writing before resubmitting.

---

◁▭▭▷ QUICK TIP ▰▰▰▰

# E-Mail with Care

Write electronic communications with the same care as all other writing. To avoid embarrassment, print a message out and edit it before hitting the "Send" button.

---

As for e-mail etiquette, if you forward material that another person has sent to you, extend the courtesy of asking the original mailer for permission. People may feel comfortable sending you an interesting article or posting, but they may not want to have their e-mail address, and taste, broadcast to others. If you are not certain how another person may react to being forwarded, and if you cannot ask permission, show cyber-courtesy and delete the screen name and other identification before forwarding.

One more important concern. Take care to double-check the e-mail address of your intended recipient. It's far too easy to click on the wrong name in your e-mail address book. Take the two or three seconds to check that the correct name appears in the "To" box, and save yourself endless embarrassment. Beyond these concerns, treat all of your electronic communication with the same care as your ordinary writing. Clear writing is mandatory for good communication.

# Appendix
# Writing Checklist

Use this checklist as your guide in turning your writing into polished prose. If you cannot answer "yes" to all of the following questions when assessing your writing, then you still have revisions to make.

## Subject

☐ Is the subject of the writing likely to be considered worth reading?
☐ Have you covered the topic fully in the space allotted to the writing?
☐ Is your handling of the subject complete?
☐ Is your information solid?

## Purpose and Audience

☐ Is your purpose clear to the reader?
☐ Does the writing accomplish your purpose?
☐ Do you know who your readers are?
☐ Will your audience understand the intention of your writing?
☐ Is the writing appropriate for the reading level of your audience?

☐ Does the writing provide enough information based on the audience's knowledge of the subject?

☐ Are your readers likely to be interested in and attentive to the writing?

# Focus

☐ Does the introduction provide readers with a clear idea of the intention of the writing?

☐ Does the introduction contain a clearly stated thesis sentence?

☐ Is the conclusion clearly related to the discussion in the body?

☐ Is the conclusion appropriate to the specific subject?

☐ Do the introduction and conclusion relate directly to the thesis sentence?

☐ Does each of the body paragraphs begin with a topic sentence that connects directly to the thesis sentence?

# Organization and Development

☐ Are all of the ideas expressed in the writing related to the thesis sentence and to each other?

☐ Is the overall structure of the writing clear to readers?

☐ Are the paragraphs placed in an effective order?

☐ Are the sentences within each paragraph organized in an effective manner?

☐ Are all of the paragraphs developed adequately?

☐ Are the body paragraphs linked by transition words and phrases?

# Content

☐ Does the writing contain sufficient specific details to support the thesis sentence?

☐ Have you given enough attention to all of the major ideas?

☐ Are irrelevant ideas avoided in the writing?

# Resources

Axelrod, Rise B., and Charles Cooper. *The St. Martin's Guide to Writing* (New York: St. Martin's Press, 2000).

Behrman, Carol. *Writing Skills Problem Solver: 101 Ready-to-Use Writing Process Activities for Correcting the Most Common Errors* (New York: Wiley, 2001).

Cockburn, Alistair. *Writing Effective Use Cases* (Reading, Mass.: Addison Wesley, 2000).

Diyanni, Robert. *The Scribner Handbook for Writers*. 3rd ed. (Boston: Allyn and Bacon, 2000).

Flesch, Rudolf. *The Art of Readable Writing* (New York: Wiley, 1994).

Raimes, Ann. *Keys for Writers: A Brief Handbook* (Boston: Houghton-Mifflin, 2001).

Rankin, Elizabeth. *The Work of Writing: Insights and Strategies for Academics and Professionals* (San Francisco: Jossey–Bass, 2001).

Strunk, William, and E. B. White. *The Elements of Style*. 4th ed. (Boston: Allyn and Bacon, 2000).

Tarshis, Barry. *Grammar for Smart People: Your User-Friendly Guide to Speaking and Writing Better English* (New York: Pocket Books, 1993).

Venolia, Jan. *Write Right! A Desktop Digest of Punctuation, Grammar, and Style* (Berkeley, Calif.: Ten Speed Press, 2001).

Walsh, Bill. *Lapsing into a Comma: A Curmudgeon's Guide to the Many Things That Can Go Wrong in Print—And How to Avoid Them* (New York: McGraw-Hill, 2000).

Worth, Richard. *Webster's New World Business Writing Handbook* (New York: Wiley, 2002).

Zinsser, William K. *On Writing Well: The Classic Guide to Writing Nonfiction*. 25th Anniversary ed. (New York: HarperResource, 2001).

# Index